The Culture of Conflict in Modern Cuba

The Culture of Conflict in Modern Cuba

Nicholas A. Robins

McFarland & Company, Inc., Publishers
Jefferson, North Carolina, and London

Library of Congress Cataloguing-in-Publication Data

Robins, Nicholas A., 1964–
    The culture of conflict in modern Cuba / Nicholas A. Robins.
      p.   cm.
    Includes bibliographical references and index.

    ISBN 0-7864-1415-4 (softcover : 50# alkaline paper)

    1. Cuba — Politics and government.   2. Culture conflict —
Cuba.   3. Elite (Social sciences) — Cuba — History.   4. Cuba —
History.   I. Title.
F1776.R595   2003
303.6'097291— dc21   2002156686

British Library cataloguing data are available

Cover photograph of Havana skyline © 1999 Eugenia Uhl

Manufactured in the United States of America

McFarland & Company, Inc., Publishers
 Box 611, Jefferson, North Carolina 28640
 www.mcfarlandpub.com

To my parents,
Robert Sidwar and Marjorie McGann Robins

Acknowledgments

This book would not have been possible without the support of many people, to whom I remain deeply indebted.

I would like to thank my colleagues at Tulane University, who were very supportive for many years, especially Eamon Kelly, William Bertrand, Richard Marksbury, Yvette Jones, Teresa Soufas, Gene Yeager, Debbie Grant, Gene D'Amour and Scott Cowen.

I would also like to extend special thanks to Robert Muse, Wayne Smith, Andrea Panaritis, Kimberly Stanton, Michael Kozak, Eric Tober, Michael Ranneberger, Andrew Cawthorne, José Ramón Cosio and John Kavulich.

I am especially indebted to others with whom I have worked closely, including Mona Schreiber, Katherine Donahue, Margarita Ahumada, Maria Fernanda Trujillo, Jenifer Thiel, Sue Ingles, Renee Sachs, Billie Banker, Sheila Favalora, Jonnie Johnson and Marshall Love.

I would also like to extend my sincere thanks for their support over the years to Karen Bracken, Holly Ackerman, Roderic Camp, Robert Bruce, Ana Lopez, Don Gatzke, Chris Dunn, Maureen Shea, Gene Cizek, Mark Thomas, Stephen Fowlkes, Ed Sherman, Jerry Speir, Oliver Houck, Guillermo Nañez, William Lennon, Sharon Courtney, Mike Strecker, Nancy Maveety, Ron King, Felipe Smith, Ted Henken, Aristides Baraya, Luz Escobar, Lilliam Zayes, Jacques Morial, Julio Guichard, Paul Yost, and Sally Grooms-Cowal.

At Duke University, I would like to thank Natalie Hartman, Orin Starn, John French, Deborah Jakubs, Rob Sikorski, Bruce Kuniholm, Hortencia Calvo and Luly Duke for all they have done to facilitate the preparation of this work.

Special thanks are also due to Charles Shapiro, Vince Mayer, Doug Barnes, Larry Corwin, Merrie Blocker, Nicole Venable, Garret Graves, Hayes Ferguson, Jim Varney, Richard Katz, Randy Poindexter, Gene Schreiber, Anthony Robins, Michael Smith, Eugenia Uhl, David Wolf,

John Redmann, Jim Mullin, Benjamin Goliwas, Jr., Chad Clanton and Yvonne del Portillo.

I would also like to thank my wife, Susan, who has been ever supportive and patient as I have gathered the material and written this book, and my parents, Robert and Majorie Robins, to whom this book is dedicated with love and thanks.

There are many people in Cuba to whom I owe immense thanks for their support and friendship over the years. Many if not all would probably prefer not to be mentioned here, but to all of my friends there I would like to say thanks, and better days are coming.

While I am indebted to all of these people, this should not be construed as an endorsement on their part of what is written here, and I remain responsible for any errors in this work.

Contents

Preface

Sitting on the seawall of Havana's Malecón on a cool, breezy December day, I was studying a map of Havana, trying to figure out how to take a new route back to my hotel, the Victoria. A clean-cut, well-dressed Afro-Cuban in his early thirties approached and asked in German if he could be of assistance. He became excited when I replied in Spanish that I was an American, not German. He switched to almost perfect English, and we began to chat about how best to get to my hotel. A few minutes into the conversation, he glanced over his shoulder, lowered his voice, and confided that in his house nearby he had a shrine to America. Would I like to see it?

I figured that he, Amaury, was either a government agent, a criminal, or did in fact have a shrine to America. Having already violated my rule of never looking at a map on the street in a foreign city, I decided to take my chances. We entered a nearby building whose stucco, unpainted in decades, had fallen off in places, and climbed several flights of gently eroded marble stairs in the cool near-darkness. Upon reaching the apartment on the top floor, I was introduced to his parents (José and Ymelda) and two younger sisters (Maria and Josefina) who, like their parents, were both surprised and delighted to receive a visitor. In the corner was a toddler. I later learned that Amaury was a widower and the girl was his, cared for by his parents. Like most Cubans, they lived crowded into a small two-room apartment.

There was indeed a shrine: a small American flag (a rare object in Cuba), a plastic souvenir-sized Statue of Liberty and some picture postcards of American cityscapes, all grouped on a shelf framed by the rabbit ears of the small television set's antenna. It was at the same time moving and sad. After paying respect to the shrine, I spent the next two hours drinking coffee and chatting about the U.S. and Cuba with Amaury's family. The father of my new friend, his smile punctuated by a single tooth, was still trying to understand why Ross Perot, clearly his favorite candidate, had not won the presidency in the last elections. Impressed by his interest in American politics, I asked him how they got their news. Amaury told me that his girlfriend worked at a hotel, and that *Time* and *Newsweek* are among the spoils smuggled out along with toothpaste and soap. I knew from my own hotel that foreign magazines were kept behind the check-in counter, sold only to foreigners.

Maria, about seventeen, was shy, but her slightly older sister was outspoken. "I love Cuba, but things never change here. I wish I were an American, to live in America at least. But what will happen if the Miami Cubans take over here?" The mother agreed, but from a different angle: "We don't get much here, but I think people in America never rest."

This was one of many colorful meetings with Cubans I had had over the years. For almost a decade I have been traveling to Cuba regularly, meeting and working with a wide variety of Cubans, official and otherwise, as well as dealing with Cuban Americans and U.S. government officials in the United States. The support of Tulane University's then president, Eamon Kelly, and vice-president William Bertrand, my studies in Latin American politics and society and my desire to develop a Cuban Studies Institute all led me to visit and stay in Cuba many times.

I learned a great deal about Cuba, about the Cuban Americans in the U.S., and about the U.S. government's policies toward that lovable, sometimes irritating, beautiful and unfortunate country. Conversational exchanges during the afternoon spent with Amaury's family exemplify four insights about Cuba which I gained over those many visits.

1. Cubans are only too aware that their country has, with very few exceptions, been under one form of tyranny or another since Columbus marveled at the parrots that darkened the Cuban sky. The course of Cuban history is one of consistency and continuity, and the centralizing, monopolistic ethos of the colonial period remains dominant, despite numerous efforts to change it.
2. Cubans hate their chains but fear to lose them. They are attracted to America, yet fear its domination.
3. Cubans and their friends and enemies both want and fear a pluralistic Cuba.
4. Cubans understand that though the Cuban Right in the United States hates Castro, it shares many of his principles and methods. Its members practice what they condemn and their triumph would install the same tyranny under a new name.

I will try to tell why I came to these conclusions, placing them in historical context.

People sometimes forget that the Cuban government is a dictatorship. To protect the Cuban people I have spent time with I have changed all the names and the identifying details of almost everyone in this book except, of course, myself and my colleagues at Tulane University. Some facts have been technically altered and events rearranged for similar reasons. For the rest, apart from the historical background, what is written here that is not recollected experience is its product, opinion. Different people have different experiences on the island. These are mine.

CHAPTER 1

From Conquistadors to Castro

The forces that define Cuba today are in many ways the same ones that have defined it for centuries. The ethos of monism, or the tendency to centralize power and to use it to repress pluralistic, divergent or dissenting impulses, was established early in Cuba's colonial history. A small (Spanish) elite used centralized power to rule for what they viewed as the common good. This common good usually coincided with their own good, and public office was often seen as both proprietary and a legitimate source of private gain. Political monopolies were reinforced by economic ones, all of which served to limit accountability, social mobility, an expectation of fair play and economic development.

In Cuba, as elsewhere in Ibero-America four hundred years ago, rulers viewed society as an organic whole whose constituent parts were united by the imperatives of order, harmony and uniformity. Experimentation, critical inquiry and compromise were antithetical to the imperatives of monism. These forces, and the limitations they place on human development, have been increasingly challenged over the last century and a half by efforts to develop a more pluralistic society. Indeed, much of the modern history of Cuba is a tale of the conflict between the ethos of monism and the ethos of pluralism. This work traces the monistic impulse, efforts to change it, and its manifestations in contemporary Cuba.

Like many visitors to this day, when Christopher Columbus alighted on Cuban soil on October 27, 1492, he confused what he found with what he wanted to find.* Believing that he was either in Japan or China, he set about collecting specimens of what he thought were cinnamon, Chinese

---

*The material for this chapter is drawn from several sources. For more detail, as well as an excellent guide to the literature and chronology, the reader is referred to Louis Perez's (cont.)

rhubarb and other plants to prove he had in fact reached the Orient. The island lacked large and obvious quantities of that most sought after of commodities, gold, but as Columbus explored the north coast, he marveled at the fine harbors, gentle people, and the exotic plants and birds. He also noted that the Indians smoked a form of cigar which they referred to as "tobaccos." Later, as settlement in the area increased, the colonists began to smoke it as well, and eventually it would make its way to the Old World, Asia and Africa.

Columbus named the island Juana, after the daughter of King Ferdinand and Queen Isabella; later the name was changed to Ferdinandina, after the King. The name that stuck, however, was Cuba, after the eastern settlement of Santiago de Cuba. Although Columbus would again visit the island, it was left in relative peace until 1511, when Diego Velásquez, acting under Diego Columbus, the son of the explorer, began to conquer it and to oversee its settlement. As the Spanish made their way westward, there was some native resistance, most notably from Indians led by Hatuey, a chieftain who, like many other natives, had fled to Cuba from the neighboring island of Hispañola, today home to Haiti and the Dominican Republic. Although Hatuey was captured and burned at the stake in 1512, other Indian rebellions followed, such as one in Caonao in 1513. By ruthlessly suppressing the rebellion in Caonao, the Spanish largely shattered the will of the natives to resist. Paralleling the defeat of most Indian resistance was the rise of new settlements on the island. Between 1512 and 1515, Governor Velásquez established the towns of Baracoa, Bayamo, Trinidad, Sancti Spíritus, Havana, Puerto Príncipe and Santiago de Cuba.

The Spanish encountered three main indigenous groups as they dominated the island. Overall, estimates of original population range from

Cuba: Between Reform and Revolution (New York: Oxford University Press, 1995). For an even more detailed bibliography, see *Cuba: An Annotated Bibliography* (New York: Greenwood Press, 1988), also by Louis Perez. Other sources include the following: Azicri, Max, *Cuba: Politics, Economics and Society* (New York: Pinter Publishers, 1988). Blank, Stephen, "The End of the Affair: Moscow and Havana, 1989–1992," in *Cuba and the Future,* edited by Donald Schulz (Westport, CT: Greenwood Press, 1994). del Aguila, Juan M., *Cuba: Dilemmas of a Revolution* (Boulder: Westview Press, 1994). Leonard, Thomas M., *Castro and the Cuban Revolution* (Westport, CT: Greenwood Press, 1999). Morison, Samuel Eliot, *Christopher Columbus, Mariner* (New York: Signet Publishers, 1985). Perez-Stable, Marifeli, *The Cuban Revolution: Origins, Course and Legacy* (New York: Oxford University Press, 1993). Robins, Nicholas, and Maria Fernanda Trujillo, "Normalized Trade Relations Between the United States and Cuba: Economic Impact on New Orleans and Louisiana" in *Cuba in Transition* (Coral Gables, FL.: Association for the Study of the Cuban Economy, 1999). Suchlicki, Jaime, *Cuba: From Columbus to Castro* (New York: Pergamon-Brassey's, 1986). For those interested in Spanish colonial administrative structures, C.H. Haring's *The Spanish Empire in America* (New York: Harbinger Books, 1963) is the classic; see also Charles Gibson, *Spain in America* (New York: Harper and Row, 1967).

16,000 to 600,000 inhabitants, although it appears that the number stood at about 110,000 at the time of the first contact with the Spanish. Among the oldest groups were the Ciboney, who lived a somewhat nomadic existence, mostly in the coastal areas, and depended on hunting and especially fishing for their sustenance. Beginning around the ninth century, however, they were progressively displaced westward, or enslaved, by the first Arawak migration to the island, that of the Sub-Tainos, who arrived from Hispañola. The Arawak were more advanced than the Ciboney, and their settlements were generally larger and concentrated in the east. They produced ceramics and practiced sedentary agriculture, cultivating manioc, corn, potatoes and other vegetables. They also cultivated cotton, which they used to weave textiles and to create what they called "hammocks," as well as lines and nets used for fishing. In addition to these fishing techniques, they also developed fish and turtle farms.

A subsequent Arawak migration had begun in the mid–1400s, and in 1500 the Arawak groups accounted for about 90 percent of the island's population. By this time the Ciboney were largely confined to the west, living in caves and subsisting on the land and sea. When the Spanish arrived, the Arawak were under increasing pressure and attack from the belligerent and cannibalistic Caribs. Although the Caribs did not settle in Cuba, frequent incursions from Hispañola and ensuing engagements led to the death of many Arawak warriors. By 1520, the native population had plummeted from around 110,000 to around 19,000, and by 1550 only about 3,000 Indians survived on the island. Despite the brutality of the conquest and the ensuing enslavement, malnutrition and often suicide of the native people, their decline cannot be attributed only to these factors. The Indian, as a source of labor, was also a source of wealth, and it was not in the interests of the colonists to exterminate them. As elsewhere in the Americas, diseases such as measles and smallpox brought by the colonists, to which the Indian had no resistance, accounted for much of the decline of the indigenous population.

The process of conquest also involved the establishment of a colonial administrative structure and the integration of the island into the mercantilist orbit of Spain. The colonial administration mirrored that found later throughout Latin America. In the case of Cuba, the king's representative was the governor, whose extensive executive, legislative, military and judicial powers were complemented by a large staff. Corregidores, or provincial governors, had similar prerogatives and reported to the governor. For most of the colonial period, the governor of Cuba was under the jurisdiction of the Viceroy of New Spain, in Mexico City, and the Audiencia in Santo Domingo in Hispañola. The Audiencia, and its members, or *oidores*, served as a court of appeal endowed with executive and investigative powers. Distance, and the time involved in covering it, however, translated into a great deal of autonomy. Much of the day-to-day administration of the colony was carried out by various lesser royal officials, many of them dealing with the *Casa de Contratación*, or House of Trade, in Seville, which was responsible for the licensing, taxation and administration of all trade between Spain and the Americas.

In the municipalities, government was administered by the *ayuntamiento*, or town council, which was also often referred to as the *cabildo*. Its members included a representative of the governor, as well as *alcaldes*, or judges, and *regidores*, or councilmen. Although much of its work was of a legislative and executive nature, it also had judicial powers. Initially the alcaldes and regidores were often conquistadors, although later they would include Creoles, or those of direct Spanish descent born in the New World. Generally, the local governor would nominate candidates based on the suggestions of outgoing regidores, although occasionally they would be named by the king. Those in the cabildo and other public offices often used their positions to obtain land or other goods and to benefit from monopolies. This tendency to see the holding of public office as both proprietary and a means to private enrichment only grew when, as early as the mid–1500s, the crown began to sell various government offices.

Intimately tied with the state was the Catholic Church. The relationship was solidified by the *patronato real*, which bound the Spanish monarchy and Vatican closely and made the Spanish king the secular leader of the Church in the American colonies. This union resulted from papal bulls in 1501 by Pope Alexander VI, and in 1508 by Pope Julius II. Together, these bulls granted the Spanish king the tithes generated in the Americas, to be used for religious purposes, and the right to establish churches, monasteries and convents and to make ecclesiastical appointments. In addition to ministering to the colonists, the Church operated the schools of the island and sought the Christianization of, and, at least initially, better treatment for the natives and slaves. As elsewhere, the confessional served not only as a means of expiation, but also on occasion as a means of uncovering planned rebellions. Over time the economic power of the Church in Cuba would grow immensely, much of its wealth deriving from bequests, taxes, rents, investments and other economic activity.

To consolidate their control over their New World possessions, and to create revenue, the Spanish established the *encomienda* system, whereby Indians were "entrusted" to a Spaniard, who had the right to their labor and was expected to Christianize them. Mass baptisms generally served the latter purpose, and the Indians were thus put at the service of their new overlords, who were known as *encomenderos*. This system, in essence one of slavery, was challenged by the Dominican Friar Bartolomé de las Casas, known as the "Protector of the Indians," who tirelessly wrote and argued for the better treatment of the Indians, most notably in his *History of the Indies*. His efforts bore fruit in 1542 when Spain issued the New Laws, which were chiefly concerned with protecting the Indians. They reaffirmed that the natives in the realm were free and prohibited the enslavement of even those captured in war. The New Laws also prohibited the practice of branding the Indians, and, most importantly, prohibited the granting of new encomiendas.

Further, royal and religious officials were to relinquish their encomiendas immediately, while all others were inheritable for only one generation, although this was sometimes extended. Recognizing the effect of the conquest on the Indian population in Cuba, the New Laws also provided that the Indians were to be subject to no more exactions than the Spanish themselves. It was, however, too little too late, as only a few thousand Indians survived in Cuba by this point.

These reforms generated a great deal of discord, and in Peru even resulted in civil war. In the end, the encomienda was not so much abolished outright as phased out, and as so often, enforcement of many of the provisions was lax. The encomienda was in the end replaced by the *repartimiento*, which put colonial authorities in charge of the distribution of mandatory labor throughout the American colonies. Humanitarian concerns were not at the forefront of the reasons for this change, however. Having struggled to unite Spain, the Crown was loath to see the rise of encomenderos as a new hereditary nobility which could further dilute and fragment the Crown's authority in the realm.

Although conditions in Cuba helped to spur the creation of the New Laws, they and the ensuing repartimiento system had fewer repercussions in Cuba than elsewhere in the Spanish realm due to the rapid decline of the native population on the island. Continuing pressure for a labor force caused an increase in the importation of black slaves mostly from Africa. As early as 1515, the Crown received a petition to import slaves to Cuba from Hispañola. Such requests continued, and, in 1526, 145 slaves arrived from the Cape Verde islands. By 1789, approximately 100,000 slaves had been imported to Cuba, by 1850 over 527,000 had been brought there. Indeed, the expansion of slavery in Cuba paralleled the development of the economy, and was central to tobacco, and later, sugar and coffee, production. Initially, however, slave labor was focused on panning for gold in the rivers of eastern and central Cuba, although by 1545 these sources were largely exhausted. Slaves were also assigned to work in other agricultural endeavors as well as in mining and construction. The more fortunate among them became domestic servants, while others fled to the interior. These latter came to be called *cimarrones*, and often joined entire villages of runaways, or *palenques*. Slave revolts were not uncommon, and became more frequent in the eighteenth century, especially on mines and plantations. Free or on the run, the Africans brought with them their religion, which over the years was gradually and partially fused with Catholicism to form Santería as it is practiced today. As in the rest of Latin America, the vast majority of colonial immigrants from Spain were male, and widespread miscegenation gave rise to a significant mulatto population.

The slaves were at the bottom of the social pyramid of colonial Cuba, which had many characteristics of a caste system. At the top were the Spaniards, or *peninsulares*. They controlled the government and much of the economy, the military and the clergy. Those born in the New World to Spanish parents, the Creoles, or *criollos*, had similar though more modest prerogatives. Although the highest positions of power were reserved for the Spanish, Creoles had an important role in the colonial political economy, and this increased as time passed. The Spaniards and Creoles formed the landed class, and owned herds of cattle and plantations for growing tobacco, and as time progressed, sugar and coffee. Other Creoles served as attorneys, accountants and merchants. The lower class was composed of mulattos, and to a lesser extent, *Mestizos*, or those of mixed Spanish and Indian heritage, and former slaves who had purchased or otherwise obtained their freedom. These groups often worked as artisans or foremen or in similar occupations. Beneath them were the few remaining Indians and the slaves.

Like many entrepreneurs who would follow them, most colonists were lured by visions of quick riches. Unlike the British and French colonists in North America, who generally came with the intent of staying, many in Cuba and elsewhere in Latin America saw a stint in the New World as temporary: they expected to return home to Spain, where they would build a large house and obtain a seat on the cabildo. Thus, to many, Cuba was just a stopping point along the way. Cuba lacked gold and silver, but its strategic position as a gateway to the Spanish dominions in America led to the early development of the island as a service and staging outpost for the larger mainland colonial enterprise. Expeditions which led to the conquest of Central America, Mexico and Florida departed from Cuba, and the discovery of gold and silver in Mexico caused many who had settled in Cuba to leave the island and go there in search of fortune. By 1544, Cuba had a population of barely over 4,400, with 660 Spaniards, 800 of their slaves, and about 3,000 Indians

By the mid–1500s, much of the economic activity on the island was devoted to the maritime service industry and to sustaining the permanent population. Early in the conquest, cattle and pigs were introduced to the island, and reproduced prodigiously in the excellent pastureland. Cattle raising was a source of salted meat and also leather, which was increasingly in demand in Europe. Despite the lack of mineral wealth on the island, the Spanish were not the only ones interested in it. Over the following years the coastal settlements were frequently attacked by British or French pirates. This problem in fact helped the development of Havana, which though founded in 1519 became the capital only in 1538. In an effort to reduce losses to piracy, the Spanish began, in the 1560s to use its harbor as a gathering point for ships sailing to and from Spain and the New World in convoy under the FLOTA, or fleet, system. The fleet system was only a component of a highly regulated trade system. Reflecting the prevailing mercantilist views of the time, all trade and related finance with the American colonies were regulated by the *Casa de Contratación*, founded in 1503. It issued regulations, collected taxes, prosecuted trade-related criminal and civil cases, and even trained ships' pilots. The only legal external trade was with Spain, and, with few exceptions, colonies were not allowed to trade with other colonies or nations for much of the colonial period.

In the 1600s tobacco exports also increased, as the taste for the leaf developed in Europe and elsewhere. By 1717 this had reached the point at which, seeing so much revenue from tobacco, the Crown established a monopoly on its trade, one that would last until 1812. The monopolistic impulse was not limited to tobacco, and in 1740 the Crown supported the establishment of the Royal Company of Commerce. All producers of sugar, tobacco and leather were required to sell their products to the Company, which purchased them at artificially low prices and then reaped the lion's share of the profits. The Company also had control over imports, which meant higher prices for such goods on the island and led to an increase in the already significant contraband trade among the European colonies in the Americas.

Indeed, throughout the colonial period, contraband trade long served as a way around colonial monopolies and had whetted the appetites of the colonists for a broader and more abundant array of goods. In 1762, the British took Havana and held it for almost a year, opening it to world trade. The Spanish had sided with the French in the Seven Years War (1756–1763), reflecting the close relations between the thrones of the two countries, as well as a fear of rising British influence in the Caribbean. Havana was held as a pawn in this conflict, and the British returned it to the Spanish in exchange for Spain's possessions in Florida under the terms of the Treaty of Paris in 1763. During the eleven months of British occupation, the fetters of Spanish mercantilism were cast off, a vast assortment of goods entered Cuba, and sugar production and exportation rose dramatically. Free trade had arrived, much of it with England and her colonies in North America. Under the British occupation, over 700 trading vessels visited Havana, more than the number that had arrived in the previous ten years. The Cubans, and the American colonies to the north, learned what they had been missing, and things would never be quite the same again.

Sugar production and exportation increased even more dramatically in 1791 with the explosion of the war of independence in Saint Domingue, the French colony which would become Haiti. This slave-led rebellion not only caused the collapse of the sugar industry in western Hispañola, but sent shock waves and fears of a race war throughout the Americas. As a result the Spanish crown relaxed many restrictions on trade and the importation of slaves in an effort to expand their share of the sugar market. The effect on sugar production was significant, raising it from 14,000 tons in 1790 to 34,000 tons in 1805. As sugar increased in economic importance to the island, smaller operations were bought and consolidated into larger ones, and, despite continuing fears of revolts, the slave trade increased significantly. About half of the slave population worked on sugar plantations, while others worked on tobacco and coffee plantations, where their life expectancy was about seven years after disembarking in Cuba. About a quarter worked in urban areas, often hired out as laborers.

By 1818, as part of a broader program of trade liberalization, Spain allowed Cuban ports to trade freely with other countries, and what was already a vibrant trade with the U.S. expanded considerably. The rise of beet sugar produced outside of Cuba, beginning in 1821, and increasing British suppression of the slave trade did, however, dampen the Cuban sugar economy. Despite the British efforts the slave trade continued in Cuba, and, by the 1840s, the decline of coffee prices led to increased sugar production and its increasing exportation to the United States. In addition, the development of railroads which could bring cane to the mills, brought new areas under cultivation. As the sugar industry expanded and that of coffee rebounded, extensive cattle ranches were increasingly sold in parcels to plantations. The rise in the number of sugar mills underscores the growth of sugar production: while in 1805 there were 478, by 1827 there were 1,000, and by 1860 the number had doubled to 2,000.

Although economic expansion did not translate into economic diversification, it did result in an increase of slave rebellions throughout the island, especially in 1812, 1826, 1830, 1835, 1837, 1840 and 1841. Increasingly, these were well-planned efforts that went beyond a single estate, often had the support of free blacks and sometimes whites, and sought both the abolition of slavery and independence. Blacks formed the majority of the population, and such uprisings, and the participation of blacks in other rebellions, were an important part of the independence struggle.

The first two decades of the nineteenth century witnessed the independence of much of Latin America, but not of Cuba. Several factors account for this. As the independence movements raged throughout the continent, many loyalists fled to Cuba. In addition, a sizable Spanish garrison helped discourage independence efforts, as did a degree of economic prosperity. Slavery was a large part of the equation as well. A fear of a slave uprising and the establishment of a black republic lurked in the minds of many Peninsulars and Creoles, and as long as Spain defended slavery, its rule was attractive to many of the elite. It is thus not surprising that, with the exception of slave rebellions, early independence efforts originated outside of the island. As early as January, 1826, Andrés Manuel Sánchez, Francisco Aguero and eight compatriots were captured and executed soon after launching an insurrection on the southern coast of Camaguey province. Other independence efforts, such as the Mexican "Great Black Eagle's Legion" and the Venezuelan Masonic "Rays and Suns of Bolívar," were among the externally backed efforts to rid the region of Spanish rule.

Just as there were pressures against Spanish rule in Cuba from other Latin American countries, there was also pressure from the United States. In 1823, John Quincy Adams, in a letter to Hugh Nelson, the U.S. Ambassador to Spain, expressed the view that the annexation of Cuba to the U.S. was "indispensable." Adams was only the first U.S. president with an interest in Cuba. In the mid 1800s, Presidents Polk, Pierce and Buchanan sought to purchase Cuba from Spain. In 1854, the U.S.-sponsored "Ostend Manifesto" again called for the purchase of Cuba, or barring that, its forcible annexation. While Adams saw the strategic importance of its location, other annexationists in the South feared, like many Cubans, that it could end up an independent nation governed by former slaves.

This led to efforts, based in the U.S., that sought Cuban independence by means other than slave revolt. Most prominent among these was that of Narciso López. Born in Venezuela, López fought on the side of the Spanish during the independence war there. Later, after moving to Cuba and marrying into a wealthy family, he became progressively alienated from the government and increasingly involved in promoting the annexation of Cuba to the U.S. As a result of this activity he was exiled to the U.S., where he continued his efforts. With the support of American southerners and some Cubans, Narciso López led two assaults on Cuba. The first, with over 600 men, departed in May, 1850, from New Orleans and landed in Cardenas. His forces took the town, but were not warmly embraced by the local population, and soon retreated back to the U.S. in the face of the arriving Spanish army. Having violated U.S. neutrality laws, he was briefly imprisoned in Savannah; once free, he returned to New Orleans to resume his efforts. In 1851, with over 400 men, he tried again, planning to link up with other rebels already on the island. As it turned out, they had rebelled earlier than planned, and López was captured soon after landing in Pinar del Rio and was subsequently garroted in Havana in September 1851. With the U.S. civil war, and the ensuing abolition of slavery there, many Cubans saw less reason to support annexation. In addition, President Lincoln disavowed any desire to annex the island.

Trade with the United States continued throughout the 1850s, much of it concentrated in the sugar industry. From 1851–55, sugar and its secondary products, such as rum and molasses, constituted 84 percent of Cuba's exports. One-third of all the island's exports went to the United States. This commerce would continue to increase, and in 1884, 85 percent of all of Cuba's exports went to the United States, including 94 percent of the sugar and molasses produced on the island. American investment paralleled and underwrote much of this growth. By 1896, American interests had invested $50 million there, much of it concentrated in sugar plantations and mills which were increasingly mechanized, but also in the tobacco, mining and railroad industries.

As the possibility of, and interest in, annexation declined in the 1860s, other Cubans sought reforms that would dilute the monistic nature of colonial rule while remaining a part of the Spanish empire. The Reform Party emerged to represent a range of interests from those simply seeking reform to those who saw it as a step towards independence or annexation to the U.S. Together, reformists sought an elimination of preferential rights for Spaniards, more open trade regulations, representation in the Spanish Cortes, or parliament, and an orderly process of abolition. In response to these pressures, the Spanish government established the Junta de Información as a vehicle for the reformists to propose their agenda. The Reformist party was elected to twelve of the sixteen seats on the commission. The Junta met between 1866 and 1867, and then issued its recommendations. Instead of accepting or negotiating them, a new, reactionary administration in Spain abolished the Junta and increased taxes and political control in Cuba.

The failure of annexationist projects and reformism, combined with the reassertion of Spanish authority, increased the appeal of independence to many. One of the most significant efforts in this regard came in October of 1868, when Carlos Manuel de Céspedes issued the "Grito de Yara," or "Cry of Yara," in which he declared Cuban independence. Born in Bayamo and educated as a lawyer in Spain, Céspedes was critical of Spanish taxation policies, corruption, the absence of free trade, and restrictions on association and expression, as well as broader Spanish political and economic prerogatives. Thus began the Ten Years War, which had people under arms from different classes and races and in the end reduced much of Cuba to ruin while still leaving it in Spanish control. Céspedes was aided militarily by Máximo Gómez, a Dominican who joined the rebellion, bringing experience gained as a leader of a guerrilla war against the Spanish in his home country. The mulatto general Antonio Maceo, the "Bronze Titan," also brought the rebels skillful leadership and numerous victories. His success, however, also heightened concerns among the planter class about black domination of the movement.

In April of 1869, the rebel forces convened the Guáimaro Assembly, which promulgated Cuba's first constitution and elected Céspedes president. The constitution provided for representative government, adult male suffrage, and an orderly process of abolition which would indemnify slave owners, and called for annexation to the United States. The Spanish soon gained the advantage on the battlefield, however, and by 1871 the rebellion was largely confined to the east. Gómez and Maceo pressed the case that the war had to push westward and have economic and military costs to Spain, while Céspedes took a more cautious approach. The participation of former slaves who were liberated in exchange for their war effort, and the extensive burning of cane fields, were to be a critical part of this program; however, this undermined their support among wealthy planters in the west to whom they appealed for support and money. Those in the west were gravely concerned about the possibility that the uprising would turn into a vengeful, even genocidal, movement that would result in their death and the establishment of a black republic.

These divisions, especially the question of the pace and manner of abolition and its relation to increasing rebel ranks and disrupting the economy, were also echoed in the leadership of the rebel movement, dividing and further weakening it. The death of Céspedes at Spanish hands in February, 1874, led to resurgent power for Gómez, who again sought to push the conflict west but did not get beyond central Cuba. The Spanish had increased their military strength considerably, and had over 90,000 troops involved in the war effort. In 1876 Gómez was forced out of the insurgent military, a result of internal divisions over tactics and the resentment among some troops that a Dominican was leading their ranks. While much of the war was fought in the eastern, and to a lesser extent, central, parts of the island, it had severe effects throughout the country as many revolutionaries set fire to their own and others' cane fields.

With the economy in ruin and, a quarter of a million people dead, and with continuing divisions within the rebel leadership and its collective failure to bring the revolution to the west of the country, the rebels signed the Pact of Zanjón in 1878. The agreement included an amnesty for rebels, emancipation for slaves who had joined the rebel cause, and several government reforms. This initially brought little more than the hope of peace, as several rebel leaders from the Ten Years War refused the terms of Zanjón. There followed the Little War, from 1879–80, led by Calixto García, Guillermo Moncada, and Antonio Maceo, who was kept on the sidelines to avoid alienating potential supporters among the white elite. The population was exhausted by a decade of war and the uprising was soon defeated by the Spanish. One of the results of the war was an increase of U.S. investment with the demise of many Creole plantation owners; and exports to the north increased with the virtual closing of the European market as a result of the rise of beet sugar production there.

Neither the Ten Years War nor the Pact of Zanjón brought emancipation to Cuba's slaves, but other forces were pushing for abolition. Among these were the growing global momentum towards the abolition of slavery and the increasing mechanization of the sugar industry. The limited growth of other labor sources, such as Chinese immigrants, also demonstrated that labor needs could be met through a wage-based system. Planters increasingly recognized that a wage system freed them from supporting year round a labor force for which the greatest demand was seasonal. They also recognized that with no slaves, there would be no slave rebellions. In November, 1879, the Spanish government abolished slavery, although emancipation was to be phased in over an eight-year period. During this time, the former slaves were required to continue working for their previous masters, receiving a modest wage in return. Many slave owners, however, opted instead to free their slaves, thus reducing their financial burdens. In the end this interim system lasted six, not eight, years, and slavery was finally abolished in October, 1886.

Among those who sought Cuba's independence in this time was José Martí, who would become Cuba's foremost hero and patriot. In 1869, when he was only sixteen, he was publishing an underground pro-independence paper, *Patria Libre* (Free Fatherland). He was subsequently caught with a subversive document and sentenced to six years of labor in prison. In 1871 his sentence was cut short and he was exiled to Spain where he continued to write pro-independence tracts and also attended Madrid and Zaragoza universities, eventually earning degrees in law and philosophy. He later moved to Mexico, where he worked as a journalist, and to Guatemala, where he taught at the Central School. Returning to Cuba in 1879, he was denied permission to practice law, and again exiled to Spain for his subversive activities.

His stay in Spain this time was a short one, and by January, 1880, he had taken up residence in New York city. Here he became even more politically active, forming the Revolutionary Committee of New York while supporting himself as a journalist. He not only traveled the United States, but also the Caribbean, in his efforts to promote the cause of Cuban independence. Martí sought not only the end of Spanish rule, but a tempering of much of its monistic legacy. He advocated the distribution of government lands to the landless, economic diversification based on agriculture, and the rise of what, today, we would call social democracy. Martí was committed to the concept of national sovereignty and feared that Cuba's dominance by Spain would be succeeded by that of the United States, stating that "all I have done up to now, and shall do hereafter, is to that end…I have lived inside the monster and know its entrails."* In 1892, he organized the Cuban Revolutionary Party, and in February, 1895, the veteran generals of the Ten Years War, Máximo Gómez and Antonio Maceo, led an uprising proclaiming Cuban independence. Martí joined Gómez in Cuba and was given the rank of Major General. Eager for battle, Martí did not last long; he was killed in action in Dos Rios on May 19, 1895.

The war continued, and as with the Ten Year War, it moved from east to west and often involved a scorched earth policy. This time, however, its leadership was from a more heterodox and less elite background. Having learned from their mistakes in the Ten Year's War, Gómez and Maceo did not hesitate to push the war west this time. The rebel army, or *mambises*, gathered strength on their westward march and by January of 1896 they were in the province of Havana, one of Spain's last redoubts. Having liberated much of Pinar del Rio province, Maceo started back east. In December, 1896, in the Punta Brava area of Havana, he was caught off guard, attacked, and killed by Spanish forces.

The Spanish took drastic measures to turn the tide that was clearly running against them. By 1897 they had fielded over 200,000 troops, at a cost of $6 million a month. The Spanish named General Valeriano Weyler governor to replace Antonio Martínez Campos, whom the Spanish felt did

*Max Azicri, Cuba: Politics, Economics and Society *(New York: Pinter Publishers, 1988), 12.*

not take a hard enough line against the rebels. Weyler wasted no time in taking the offensive, and soon began forcibly concentrating civilians throughout Cuba in areas where they would be under the watchful eye of loyalist troops. Further reinforcements of fresh Spanish troops made headway against the rebels, but dominance eluded them. In 1898, believing victory was within reach, Gómez, along with Calixto García and other rebel leaders, rejected a Spanish offer of autonomy.

As early as 1896, the U.S. congress had recognized Cuba's right of self-determination and independence, and in 1898 the U.S. sent troops to Cuba. Not only did the U.S. want to see the region free of Spanish presence; it also wanted to protect US investments in the region. Cuba also had strategic value given its location in the Caribbean, something that had only grown in importance as the U.S. developed militarily and to expand its influence in the region. Many in the U.S. were divided over other objectives of the intervention, some hoping that it would be the their edge of the wedge leading to U.S. control over the island, while others were sympathetic to the Cuban cause. In either case, the departure of the Spanish would open up additional investment opportunities for American companies. The mood in the U.S. was also ripe for intervention, as "yellow journalism" had aroused the American public with tales of Spanish atrocities. The sinking of the U.S. battleship *Maine* in Havana harbor in February, 1898, with the loss of 260 lives, served as a catalyst. The U.S. entered the war in July, 1898; by December of the same year, not only was Cuba under U.S. control, but also were Puerto Rico, the Philippines and Guam. Despite his untiring efforts over the years to create an independent Cuba, General Calixto García and his troops were excluded from the American victory celebrations in Santiago de Cuba; neither he nor any other Cuban generals were involved in the 1898 Treaty of Paris which ended the war between the U.S. and Spain.

Following the American intervention in the war came U.S. military rule from January, 1899, to May, 1902, first under General John R. Brooke and then, beginning in December, 1899, under General Leonard Wood. That this was not seen as a short-term commitment on the part of the U.S. was evident in an amendment to a bill offered by Senator Orville Platt which granted the U.S. "the right to intervene for the preservation of life, property, and individual liberty." In June, 1901, after contentious debate, the Cuban Constitutional Convention ratified the Platt Amendment, with a vote of sixteen in favor, eleven opposed and four abstaining. Such intervention remained part of official U.S. policy until May 1934, when President Franklin Roosevelt rescinded that article of the amendment. Another article of the Platt amendment, however, continued in force: that which concerned the U.S. military base at Guantánamo Bay. Initially the U.S. had sought four bases on the island; after negotiation, Cuba and the United States agreed that there would be one forty-five-square-mile base, the lease on which had no expiration date and would cost the U.S. $2,000 per year.

With close political relations came close economic ties. In 1903 the two countries signed the Commercial Treaty of Reciprocity, in which Cuban sugar was granted a 20 percent reduction of tariffs, and which also gave American products better access to Cuba. As Cuban sugar poured out, American capital poured in, much of it in sugar, tobacco, mining, banking, light manufacturing, real estate and infrastructure such as railroads, ports, electricity, gas and communications. By 1905, 60 percent of the Cuban countryside was owned by American companies or individuals, and another 15 percent by Spanish interests. In 1895 U.S. direct investment in the island was about $50 million; by 1909 it had quadrupled. It continued to increase reaching about $1.3 billion in 1929. After declining during the Depression, it had again reached about that level by 1958. The U.S. presence on the island did lead to improvements in public health, sanitation, education, infrastructure and administration. Although such improvements were welcome, they were accomplished with Cuba still subject to a foreign power and still longing for independence.

In 1902, the Cuban republic was born as Cubans promulgated their first constitution and elected their first president, Tomás Estrada Palma. The constitution was patterned after that of the U.S., with a presidential system and separation of powers. As elsewhere in Latin America, the early republican period demonstrated, that the constitution was more an expression of ideals than a document that would be closely adhered to. Political structures do not in and of themselves change political culture, especially one developed over four centuries. Corruption and fraudulent elections and efforts to perpetuate one's rule were still the order of the day.

The newly elected President Estrada had been head of the Cuban Revolutionary party in New York, and had lived there for many years. Importantly to the U.S., he was pliable, and had the support of the moneyed and landed interests in Cuba. U.S. opposition had caused a more popular candidate and veteran of the Ten Year War, General Bartolomé Masó, to withdraw his candidacy. Estrada sought reelection in 1906, prompting an uprising by the Liberal party. To quell the unrest, the Platt Amendment was invoked to allow a second U.S. intervention, which lasted from 1906 to 1909. During this time Cuba was ruled by an American civilian, Charles Magoon, whose freewheeling spending and readiness to dispense sinecures failed to differentiate him from many other leaders who would follow. The

U.S. intervened by sending troops or demonstrating naval might again in 1912, 1917–20, and in 1933–34.

In January, 1909, Magoon handed over power to General José Miguel Gómez of the Liberal party, who had been elected president. Elections became a feature of the political landscape, although they were often not without controversy. In 1912, General Mario García Menocal was elected president, and another Liberal rebellion in 1917, and reelected in 1916, surviving another liberal rebellion in 1917. García may have wished he had quit while he was ahead, because the economy plummeted with the price of sugar during much of his second term. After climbing from 1.9 cents in 1914, the world price of sugar peaked at 22.5 cents a pound in May, 1920 before falling to 3.8 cents in December of the same year. This not only devastated the Cuban economy but also led to much social unrest.

In 1920, Alfredo Zayas of the Liberal party was elected and became Cuba's second civilian president. His term was characterized by attempts to revitalize the economy, and he yielded to strong and direct U.S. pressure for electoral reforms to reduce fraud, efforts to bring the budget in line with resources, and the reduction of the size of the bureaucracy. Poor economic performance and continuing U.S. involvement in government decisions heightened many people's awareness that Cuba had a long way to go to achieve self-determination. Reflecting this, the 1920s saw increasing nationalism, much of it led by student groups such as the University Students Federation, labor groups, communists and intellectuals such as Enrique José Varona and Fernando Ortíz. They reintroduced Martí's ideals, were critical of continued American political and economic involvement in the island, and sought to delegitimize a venal political establishment. Zayas sought to strengthen his position vis á vis the Americans by fanning the flames of nationalism, one result of which was the definitive return of Cuban sovereignty to the Isle of Pines, presently the Isle of Youth.

Civilian rule was not to become the norm, however, and in 1925 General Gerardo Machado of the Liberal party was elected president. Combining public works projects and nationalism, he initially embodied the hope of many Cubans for a better future. In 1928, with the support of a loyal congress, he was reelected, to a six-year term. Unopposed in a fraudulent election, he was increasingly opposed in the streets. As opposition grew, and the Great Depression set in, he became increasingly repressive, something which only precipitated further unrest. In his effort to quell dissent, Machado expelled foreign labor organizers, shuttered newspapers opposed to him, and closed the university from 1930–33. Opposition to his rule, much of which was led by students, became increasingly violent and strikes and protests led to assassinations of, and by, government officials.

Overall, the opposition was often united only in their desire to remove Machado. The students were primarily grouped in the Student Directorate, which was moderate and generally of middle class origins, and in the more radical Student Left Wing. The Masonic, middle class, cell-based ABC, established in 1931, called for agrarian reform, workers rights, the vote for women, limits on foreign investment and state control over public services. The Communist party, which was organized as the Communist Revolutionary Union and took its directions from Moscow, grew as Machado repressed labor groups. Rural unrest also grew, and smoke again rose from the cane fields as opposition groups sabotaged the economy and rail and communications facilities. Military governors were appointed in many provinces as constitutional rights were suspended throughout the island; a state of siege was declared, and civilians were increasingly judged in military courts. Others were simply abducted by the secret police, tortured and executed. In August, 1933, the opposition forces organized a general strike. The Communist party initially supported the strike, but backed off when Machado offered to release jailed communist leaders and to legalize the party. Not only did the strike go on, irrespective of the directives of the Communist party, but the communists long suffered the taint of collaboration with the Machado regime, as well as with others that would follow. Facing the general strike, continuing and widespread social unrest, and the loss of support from both the Cuban armed forces and U.S. government, Machado stepped down in 1933.

Just as the independence war had been the crucible of leadership for many who would be involved in politics in Cuba's early national period, so did the events leading to the ousting of Machado produce a second generation of leaders. The forces arrayed against Machado reflected the differentiation that society had undergone in the previous decades. The growth of the state, and its role in expanding public works, had given rise to a bureaucracy and an incipient middle class. Limited economic diversification also had led to a larger role by trade unions. Students from differing backgrounds increasingly attended the university and, upon graduation, found opportunities lacking and their expectations unmet. Although now free of Spanish domination, Cuba's colonial heritage persisted. Centralized power, attempts to establish and perpetuate political monopolies, elite rule, repression, intolerance of dissent, the use of the state for private enrichment, and advancement on the basis of personal contacts over ability continued to characterize the Cuban polity. But this ethos was increasingly confronted by another, often though not always led by individuals from the middle and lower classes. This force sought political pluralism, honesty and accountability in government, checks on power, social mobility, and policies promoting economic and political nationalism. Under Machado, the confrontation between the monistic tradition and modernity become starkly clear.

The son of the original leader of the Ten Years War, Carlos Manuel de Céspedes Quesada, was appointed provisional president with support from the ABC organization, but he served only a few weeks before being forced out by a rebellion of non-commissioned military officers led by Fulgencio Batista, a stenographer. Batista expressed the frustration of many soldiers concerning issues of pay, housing and promotion. Their rebellion, which initially had limited objectives, was supported by civilians opposed to Céspedes who leveraged it into a coup. Batista's star was now fast rising, and as a result of the rebellion he was promoted from sergeant to general and Chief of the Army. Ramón Grau San Martín, a university professor, was named provisional president in September. Grau wasted no time in advancing a nationalist and populist agenda. He and his Interior Minister, Antonio Guiteras, promulgated laws establishing an eight-hour work-day, granting permanent usufruct rights to peasants on seized lands, and limiting real estate purchases by non-nationals. In addition, he mandated that 50 percent of all employees in many enterprises be of Cuban nationality, and, in an attempt to limit communist influence in the labor movement, that union leaders be Cuban citizens. Other reforms included the abolition of the traditional political parties, the reduction of utility rates, female suffrage, and a minimum wage for those working the sugar cane plantations.

More important, Grau abrogated the 1901 Constitution, and thus Cuba's recognition of the Platt Amendment, and set up a constituent convention scheduled for April, 1934. Reflecting the importance of student support in his rise to power, Grau met their demands for university autonomy. Emboldened and encouraged by Grau's populism, strikes, land invasions and worker takeovers of sugar mills became commonplace. The elite was alienated and the U.S. refused diplomatic recognition of the regime. The regime was further plagued by divisions between Grau and Guiteras, and had only factional military support.

During this period, General Batista formed ties with the U.S. ambassador, Sumner Wells, and was soon in the position of kingmaker. In January of 1934, Batista withdrew military support of the Grau regime, forcing the president's resignation and his replacement by Carlos Mendieta of the Nationalist Union. U.S. recognition followed, and over the next six years several presidents served essentially at Batista's pleasure. In 1935 José Barnet became president, to be replaced the following year by Miguel Mariano Gómez. Between 1936 and 1940 Federico Laredo Brú served as Batista's satrap. Batista was not blind to the appeal of Grau's reforms, nor to the need for U.S. recognition. He combined tepid populism with a strong dose of corruption and, whenever necessary, repression. During this time, governments introduced reformist labor legislation, broadened the education system and passed laws strengthening the rights of tenant farmers. As a result, the regimes mollified the working and rural classes while further isolating the left.

In 1939, Batista called for the drafting of a new constitution. Despite his efforts to the contrary, over half the delegates to the constituent assembly came from parties opposed to him, such as the Auténtico, Liberal and Communist parties. The result was the Constitution of 1940, patterned to some degree after that of Mexico of 1917. It called for a high degree of state involvement in the economy, established minimum wages and pensions, enshrined university autonomy, gave the vote to all adult Cubans and guaranteed the right of political organization and other civil liberties. In addition, it prohibited consecutive reelection of the president and placed limits on large landholdings and foreign ownership of land. Overall it sought the creation of a pluralistic, liberal democracy led by a state actively involved in the economy. Like many constitutions in Latin America, however, it would turn out to be more of a statement of ideals than a working document, due in no small part to its conflicting goals.

Following the promulgation of the new constitution, Batista, with the support of the communists, won the elections of 1940, which were largely honest and fair. The increase in the price of sugar due to World War II helped the economy, and the development of the finance sector helped diversify the economy to compensate for the reduction of imported goods. This, and enabling legislation associated with the constitutional reforms, allowed some of the benefits to trickle down to the middle and lower classes, although inflation did limit these advances. Batista's rule saw the establishment of new unions, as well as pension and insurance programs. In the countryside, the number of rural schools was expanded and tenant farmers' rights were strengthened. The student movement had lost much of its momentum, and there were few to fill the shoes of the "Generation of 1930." The relative social peace which ensued also allowed Batista to keep military involvement in politics to a minimum. Despite this, the legacy of governmental corruption continued unabated.

Batista relinquished the presidency in 1944, upon the election of Grau San Martín on the Cuban Revolutionary party (Auténtico) ticket. Founded in 1934, the Auténticos combined economic and political nationalism with criticism of military involvement in politics. Although they rejected the concept of class struggle, they called for a strong state role in the economy.

These views appealed to the urban and rural working classes, some of the middle class, and, reflecting the party's origins in the university, many intellectuals and students. After his election, Grau returned from Miami where he had been living in exile, to be sworn in. If populist reforms characterized Grau's first administration, widespread corruption, scandal, mismanagement and increasing violence characterized the second. Gangs, or private militias, which often operated as armed wings of political factions, became imbedded in the political landscape and were the enforcers of competing monistic impulses. Often, they were based on the university campus, protected from police interference by its autonomy. Many gangsters were also on the official government payroll, and were used by the administration to enforce legislation and limit communist influence. Not only did these gangs serve as political enforcers, but they also often fought with each other. Having learned from the ouster of Grau in 1934, the Auténticos did not allow their nationalist rhetoric to jeopardize the larger political equation in which they operated, one which included significant U.S. direct investment and continuing influence. Thuggery mitigated the effects of numerous scandals, and Carlos Prio Socarrás, a former student leader and also an Auténtico, was elected in 1948.

Although they won the election, the party had suffered a split in 1947, with the establishment of the Cuban People's (Ortodoxo) party. Led by Eduardo Chibás, it called for honest government and economic and political nationalism, and appealed to generally the same political base that had supported the Auténticos. The public frustration with corruption and violence among the political class reflected a larger sense of disillusionment with the political process as a whole. Chibás' ceaseless attacks on the Auténticos created a large and devoted following and imbued his supporters with a firm sense of mission. In August, 1951, however, after his regular radio address, he committed suicide, leaving a void in the Ortodoxo leadership. There were many contenders to fill it. The population was increasingly alienated by a government that had relied on coercion to perpetuate its members' use of the system for their own ends; and the void in the Ortodoxo leadership created new opportunities, though not just for Ortodoxos. As preparations got underway for the 1952 elections, among the candidates for the House of Representatives was an Ortodoxo by the name of Fidél Castro. Batista, concerned that he would not win the presidency in 1952, and sensing the opportunities presented by the political situation, seized power in March of that year. Claiming he was acting to prevent Prio from extending his rule, Batista promised elections in 1954.

Initially, his coup was welcomed by many, including the working classes, who had grown tired of the mismanagement and corruption of the Auténticos. While some hoped for a reduction in violence and lawlessness, others, such as the Communist party, which in 1944 was renamed the Popular Socialist party, breathed a sigh of relief with the demise of their political nemesis. Overall, the coup generated little resistance, either civil or from institutions such as the Catholic Church. This would, however, change in the years to come. As in his previous administrations, Batista sought to strengthen his support not only among the elite and business interests, but also among blue collar workers and the rural classes. Batista's rule from 1952 through 1958 did result in some economic growth. The mining sector, especially that concerned with the extraction of nickel and cobalt, expanded, as did cattle ranching, and there was a focused effort to develop tourism. Despite this, sugar and foreign capital continued their preeminent role in the economy. Between 1949 and 1958 sugar and its byproducts were responsible for approximately 30 percent of the GNP, and 85 percent of exports. These exports, mostly to the U.S., were dependent on allowances of the U.S. sugar quota, which were obtained by preferential tariffs for U.S. goods entering Cuba. What was good for sugar exports was deleterious to the Cuban manufacturing sector, however. During this period, about 65 percent of Cuban products were exported to the U.S., and approximately 75 percent of Cuba's imports were American.

Batista did hold elections in 1954, but he was the only presidential candidate. His rule increasingly echoed, and then exceeded, that of the Auténticos in its use of repression.

Censorship became widespread, and opponents were jailed, exiled or killed.

As they did with Machado, the students, affiliated with the major political parties and protected by university autonomy, again raised the banner of resistance, especially after 1955. By this time demonstrations and violent confrontations with the police and army were commonplace. Batista had long been an authoritarian populist. During his rule from 1940–44, it was primarily his populist tendencies which were evident, now it was increasingly the opposite.

One of the earliest challenges to Batista's rule came on July 26, 1953. Fidél Castro, his brother Raúl and 150 other rebels attacked the Moncada barracks in the city of Santiago de Cuba, hoping to spur a larger uprising by Ortodoxo military officers and to force Batista to resign. Although it resulted in the death of many rebels and the capture of the others, the audacity of the attack and the publicity which ensued brought Fidél Castro to the forefront of the opposition movement. This prominence was further solidified when Castro, an attorney, made a famous speech in his own defense in which he asserted that "History will absolve me." Despite the efforts of the Batista regime to prevent the circulation of an edited version of the speech, its ideas became a rallying point for many who opposed the regime. What is most notable is the moderate nature of the ideas presented: Castro demanded adherence to the 1940 constitution, prosecution of corrupt politicians and agrarian reform.

Although sentenced to fifteen years in jail for the Moncada attack, Castro spent only the next year and a half in prison, in the Isle of Pines, off the southwest coast of Cuba. During his time there he developed his knowledge of Marxism, read the works of Martí, and planned for the future. In 1955, as a result of an amnesty, Castro and many others were released from prison. Upon his release he relocated to Mexico, where he established the July 26 movement (M-26-7), so named in commemoration of the date of the Moncada attack. It sought to continue the work of Chibás, the founder of the Ortodoxos, but now through the bullet and not the ballot box. As Castro developed the July 26 Movement, he came in contact with Ché Guevara, an Argentine physician. Castro also developed his contacts in Cuba, especially with the Revolutionary Directorate (DR), a largely middle-class splinter group of the University Students Federation which sought a return to constitutional rule. Although the DR and Castro had wide differences, in 1956 they signed the Pact of Mexico, calling for an armed uprising to oust Batista. The urban terrorism of the DR would soon be complemented by that of urban cells of the July 26 Movement. This came about with the merging in 1955 of the Eastern Revolutionary Action group, led by Frank País and others, into the July 26 Movement.

A year later, in December, 1956, Castro and 81 fellow revolutionaries left Mexico on board the pleasure yacht Granma, disembarking in Cuba on December 2, 1956. Their arrival was coordinated with attacks on military installations, railroads and electrical service. As it turned out, poor weather was the least of their worries, as, acting on intelligence he had received, Batista surprised the rebels. Of the 81 who landed, 18 managed to escape into the Sierra Maestra mountains of eastern Cuba. Batista's assertion that Castro had been killed was disproved when *New York Times* reporter Herbert Matthews interviewed the rebel leader in February, 1957. Castro played the moderate card, vowing to restore democracy to Cuba and asserting that he bore no grudge against the Americans. By having his limited troops always on the move during the interview, he was able to convince Matthews that his forces were much stronger than they in fact were. A few months later the rebels released their manifesto, *Nuestra Razón*, "Our Purpose," in which, spiced with quotes from Thomas Jefferson and Abraham Lincoln, they called for a politically and economically nationalist, democratic, pluralistic government which would uphold individual liberties. It rang much more of Martí than Marx, and in many respects reflected Ortodoxo principles.

In addition to armed uprisings, there were also peaceful attempts to persuade Batista to step down. Most prominent among these were the efforts of the Society of the Friends of the Republic (SAR). The SAR was composed of a broad array of political and civic actors, ranging from Auténticos to students to radicals, and sought to negotiate Batista's exit through elections. In the end, Batista turned down their recommendations and the efforts of the SAR only demonstrated the futility of dialogue. The result was that many moderates began to see an armed uprising as perhaps the only means of removing Batista.

The revolution continued to spread in both the countryside and cities. In March, 1957, members of the DR attacked the presidential palace and a radio station. Despite deaths on both sides, Batista escaped unscathed. In response, he unleashed harsh repressive measures against the opposition and hunted down DR members. Although the DR continued to be active, its fragmentation and internal divisions limited its future impact. Other groups, such as the Civic Resistance Movement and armed factions of the Auténticos continued to engage in urban terrorism and kidnappings. The repressive response such attacks engendered only further alienated the middle classes, and in the end their support for Castro was critical in overthrowing the regime.

Batista became increasingly isolated, remaining unresponsive to increasingly strident calls from business leaders and the Catholic Church for a negotiated end to the regime. He was now on a downward curve, made steeper by the establishment of a U.S. arms embargo on the country in March, 1958, as part of a strategy to pressure him to hold elections and transfer power. Many in the U.S. State Department were ambivalent about Castro, unsure if he was a radical revolutionary or a moderate forced to take up arms. Such ambivalence was also being played out in the rebel ranks, as different tendencies vied for dominance among various leaders, such as Ché Guevara and René Ramos Latour, the latter of the July 26 Movement urban underground. For his part, Castro mostly stayed out of these debates, sensing that his, and the movement's, interests were best served by efforts to appeal to the broadest range of social sectors possible. Castro continued his efforts from the mountains, seeking to dominate the opposition and the government by attacking military installations and destabilizing the economy in the east. Initially, his hope was that a general strike and popular insurrection would serve to oust Batista. When mass riots did not happen, and a general strike failed in April, 1958, it became clear to him that military means and economic sabotage were the paths to victory.

Throughout the insurrection, the Communist party had remained largely irrelevant to the events around it. Although persecuted by the Auténticos, it had cooperated with Machado in his final hour, and communists had served in Batista's cabinet in his first administration. It was not only small and Stalinist, but its cooperation with various governments had discredited it and its members remained uninvolved in the insurgency. Indeed, the party had criticized the Moncada attack in 1953, and the occasional strike was the extent of its resistance to the Batista dictatorship. Reflecting its political status and relevancy at the time, its membership plummeted from about 20,000 in 1952 to under 4,000 six years later. It was only in the final stretch of the insurrection, in late 1958, that the communists sought a role in the uprising.

Time was running out for Batista, and, despite increasingly brutal repression, his rule began to unravel. A concerted offensive against the rebels in mid–1958 exposed the weakness of his regime rather than demonstrating its strength. The morale of field-level officers and their troops suffered as a result of their engagements with the rebels and numerous uprisings and acts of sabotage throughout the island, and a general belief that the game was up. Military conspiracies by disgruntled younger officers abounded, and in November, with rebels under Ché Guevara and Camilo Cienfuegos operating in the Escambray mountains, the U.S. Ambassador told Batista that the U.S no longer would support his administration. In December, a military coup led by General Eulogio Cantillo overthrew Batista, and on January 1, 1959, he fled the country. In the face of a general strike, the military government, now led by Colonel Ramón Barquín, surrendered to the rebel army.

On January 8, Castro arrived victorious in Havana and quickly filled the power vacuum left by Batista: not only had the rebel army developed an aura which appealed to many, it was also the best organized and most disciplined of the opposition forces. Initially, Castro served as the head of the army, and endorsed the appointment of Manuel Urrutía as president. Urrutía quickly dissolved congress and dismissed all governors, mayors and city councils and removed all Batista supporters from the bureaucracy. Many of the old guard were executed after brief trials before revolutionary tribunals. In February Castro became Prime Minister; in October, he dismissed Urrutía and appointed the former Communist party leader Oswaldo Dorticós in his place. Castro enacted sweeping reforms, which included land expropriations and reductions of urban rents. The Agrarian Reform Law caused considerable concern in Washington, which would only grow. In February, 1960, the signing of a trade agreement with the Soviet Union and the establishment of the Central Planning Board initiated Soviet subsidies and centralized economic planning. This both underscored and furthered the growing division between the U.S. and Cuba.

The Soviet agreement provided for exchanges of Soviet oil for Cuban sugar, a practice that would continue for many years. In June, 1960, however, American owned companies in Cuba refused to process the Soviet oil, and Castro responded by nationalizing them. The U.S. retaliated the following month by eliminating the Cuban sugar quota. The following months saw the further nationalization of American interests on the island, including sugar mills, electric and telephone companies, banks and real estate. In October, 1960, the U.S. imposed a trade embargo on the island, and in January of 1961 the two countries broke diplomatic relations. Castro's actions had demonstrated the ideological orientation of the revolution, and in April, 1961, he announced that the revolution was Socialist. In December of the same year, he announced that he was a Marxist-Leninist.

There is ongoing debate as to whether Castro had long been a communist, or if the U.S. somehow pushed him into it and the arms of the Soviet Union. What is clear is that he kept his cards close to his fatigues, even in the Sierra Maestra. He had exposure to Falangist ideas in secondary school, and read Marx widely when in prison. It may be that what appealed to him was totalitarianism, and the Soviets were in a position to aid him in establishing it on the island. This was despite assertions to the contrary, during the guerrilla phase, when in an effort to gain the critical support of the middle classes he promoted a moderate line based on the restoration of the 1940 constitution. To insist that the U.S. "pushed" him into communism ignores his totalitarian affinities and also suggests that he was incapable of making independent decisions. Whatever the case, Castro lost little time in concentrating political power in his own hands and economic power in those of the state — and thus also in his.

Castro was slow to institutionalize his rule, and when doing so was careful that such a process would enhance, not dilute, his power. Like many leaders before him, though to a much greater degree, he instituted a system that appeared different yet remained staunchly monistic. He began the process in 1961, when he united the three main revolutionary groups into the Integrated Revolutionary Organizations, or ORI. This brought together the July 26 Movement, which Castro had led; the Revolutionary Directorate, composed of students of the University of Havana; and the communist Popular Socialist Party. In 1963, the ORI became the United Party of the Socialist Revolution (PURS), and two years later it was renamed the Cuban Communist Party (PCC). Paralleling these developments was the establishment of numerous mass organizations under government control, such as those composed of women, students and farmers. In addition, in 1960 the government established the Committees for the Defense of the Revolution, (CDR), a massive organization on every block in every neighborhood, as well as in rural areas, designed to detect and prevent counterrevolutionary activity and ensure compliance with government directives.

Rallies, and mass mobilizations through "brigades," soon became a currency of the revolution. Perhaps the most notable of the latter was the literacy campaign of 1961, which over the course of a year reduced illiteracy from 20 percent of a population of seven million to about 4 percent. Opportunities to apply the benefits of widespread literacy were limited, however. Intellectual and cultural life quickly became subject to very clearly delineated parameters. This was perhaps most succinctly expressed by Castro in June of 1961, when at a meeting of artists and intellectuals at the National Library, he in effect gave them their marching orders with a now-famous quotation: "Within the revolution, everything, against the revolution, nothing." In addition to literacy, the government made strides in expanding the availability of healthcare to, and significantly reducing malnutrition among, the population.

The revolution also created new relations between the state and the Catholic Church. Although the church did not support the various independence movements of the 1800s, it initially did support Castro's revolution. As the nature of the changes instituted by the revolutionary government became more evident, however, antagonistic relations prevailed and the influence of the church was soon all but eliminated from national life. The fact that communism is a secular religion, and totalitarian in nature, goes a long way to explaining why as a system it does not tolerate other, competing sources of social influence. While the restructuring of the educational system in the early revolutionary period reduced the role of the Catholic Church in society, the involvement of priests in counterrevolutionary activities served as an additional pretext for the government to further consolidate power. It should be recognized, however, that even before 1959 Catholicism did not dominate Cuban society to the degree found in many other Latin American countries. This can be largely attributed to the important influence of Santería, the Afro-Cuban religion with Yoruba roots in Nigeria. By the early 1960s, 90 percent of the nuns and over 60 percent of the priests had left the country. Although smaller in numbers, Protestant pastors and Jewish rabbis also experienced similar declines.

President John Kennedy soon went further than an embargo in trying to oust Castro, and under CIA direction trained a group of Cuban exiles in Florida and Guatemala to invade the island. Departing from Puerto Cabezas, Nicaragua, they attempted to establish a beachhead in the Bay of Pigs in April, 1961. Of the 1,500 exiles of the "2506 brigade" who landed, 1,113 were captured by the Cuban military within two days. The exiles were left in the lurch, as Kennedy decided, after the invasion was underway to withhold the promised American air support. Neither does it seem that the time was ripe, as at that early stage the revolution did enjoy considerable popular support. Many had invested effort and hope in the revolution, and believed it would bring them a better future. The captured exiles would eventually make it back to the U.S., on December 24, 1962, when, after extensive negotiations, American corporations paid Castro's government $54 million in pharmaceuticals and baby food. Among the results of the Bay of Pigs was the recognition by the Soviet Union that the U.S. lacked the political will to eliminate the regime. The Soviets did, however, harbor reservations over Castro's personalistic style of leadership and his frictions with the Communist party. Among these were Castro's insistence on the greater importance of armed struggle in Latin America and elsewhere versus the leading role of the Communist party as the path to communism. Nevertheless, the Soviets now saw that the road was clear for greater economic and military involvement in Cuban affairs.

The confrontation with the United States took on a new dimension in October, 1962, when the world came to the brink of nuclear war during the Cuban missile crisis. The Soviet Union had located intermediate range ballistic missiles (IRBMs) on the island, as much, if not more, to balance a similar threat posed by the U.S. in Turkey and Italy than to defend their new satellite state. Tensions escalated as the U.S. placed a naval blockade on the island, intercepting every ship which sought to enter Cuban waters and searching it for weapons. Eventually, Premier Khrushchev agreed to remove the missiles and bring them back to the Soviet Union on the condition that the U.S. pledge not to invade Cuba and to dismantle U.S. missiles in Turkey. Castro opposed, and in the end resented, the removal of the missiles, and for having been largely shut out of the negotiations.

Time has shown that centralized economic planning yields poor results, and Cuba is no exception to the rule. The heady optimism of the early 1960s quickly gave way to shortages, rationing, continued dependence on sugar production, a growing external debt to the Soviet Union, high absenteeism and the use of moral, as opposed to material, incentives to work harder. Seeking to generate the capital to make a shift to a more industrially oriented economy, Castro developed the Ten Million Tons campaign in which he sought to increase sugar production to this level in 1970. The military was mobilized to assist the effort, city people were sent to the countryside for the arduous task of cutting cane, and many other resources were reoriented towards attaining the goal. When all was said and done, the harvest was 8.5 million tons, and many other sectors of the economy had suffered as a result of the redirection of resources. What amounted to an embarrassing defeat spurred Castro to further institutionalize and somewhat decentralize the regime in the coming years and to adhere more closely to Soviet directives concerning economic policy as a condition for continuing financial assistance.

The final result of this process of institutionalization was the 1976 Cuban constitution, based largely on that of the Soviet Union. Among the changes were the establishment of Organs of People's Power (OPPs), which were legislative bodies at the local, provincial and national levels. Delegates were elected, from the Communist party, directly at the municipal level. Municipal representatives then elected representatives for the fourteen provincial assemblies and the 481 representatives of the National Assembly, which meets for a few days twice a year. Prior to the establishment of the OPPs, all executive, judicial and legislative functions had been concentrated in the Council of Ministers, established in 1959. New administrative mechanisms should, however, not be confused with any meaningful dilution of power. The Executive Committee of the Council continues to run the show, and Fidel and Raúl Castro are its president and vice-president, respectively.

In Cuba, the 1970s brought some, albeit inconsistent, economic growth, much of it the result of high sugar prices and Soviet subsidies. The nationalization of small businesses which had heretofore escaped being "collectivized" further stifled growth and alienated many. As early as 1961, education, the financial sector and much commerce had been nationalized. Capping a continuing process, the "Revolutionary Offensive" of 1968 brought all remaining retail commerce directly under government control, as well as all construction and industrial enterprises. One of the results of this nationalization, which included 56,000 small businesses, was the expansion of black market activity. Socially, the 1960s and 1970s also saw increases in both the marriage and divorce rates in Cuba. While the marriage rate doubled, that of divorce jumped 800 percent. This partially reflected social changes whereby women adopted new, non-traditional roles, which many men were reluctant to accept.

The Castro government has long sought to export revolution to other countries, and to have a leadership role in international affairs. The government provided training and often material and other support to guerrilla movements in Bolivia, Nicaragua, El Salvador, Colombia and other countries. In Africa, it has been more directly involved. As early as 1963, Cuban troops were sent to support Algeria during the Algerian-Moroccan war, and in 1965, Ché Guevara was fighting a losing battle in the Congo. In 1975, fighting as a Soviet proxy in Angola, Cuba sent troops to aid the Popular Movement for the Liberation of Angola. In all, over 18,000 Cuban troops served in Angola. Cuba also sent 16,000 troops to Ethiopia in 1978 to buttress Soviet support of the leftist government of Mengistu Haile Marian. Even greater numbers of Cuban civilians were sent to both countries as well. The government also supported the Patriotic Front in Zimbabwe and the South West People's Organization in Namibia. Cuba's involvement as a founding member of the Non-Aligned Nations movement since its first conference in 1961 has also served as a platform for the government to express its ideological views. This was especially pronounced when Castro became head of the movement in 1979, serving for just over three years. His obvious alignment with the Soviet Union, and his failure to condemn the Soviet invasion of Afghanistan in 1979, significantly limited and undermined his credibility in this regard.

Apart from coercion, one of the factors which facilitated both the consolidation and the durability of the revolution was emigration. Between January, 1959, and November, 1965, over 183,000 Cubans entered the United States, often settling in Florida. Many of these were educated professionals who had formed the upper and middle classes of pre–Revolutionary society. In the following years, hundreds of thousands more would follow in their footsteps. Between 1966 and 1973, an additional 260,000 Cubans left their homeland, aided by a 1965 Memorandum of Understanding between Cuba and the U.S. This accord provided for an airlift service between Varadero and Miami. When this arrangement ended in 1973, emigration decreased abruptly, and from 1973 to early 1980, about 34,000 Cubans came to the U.S. This changed dramatically, however, in 1980, with the Mariel boatlift, named for the port of embarkation for the émigrés. Despite the earlier mass exodus, many Cubans who had remained were disaffected and wanted out. Between April and September of 1980, over 125,000 Cubans came to America, while others went to Costa Rica and other countries. Overall, emigration has served as an escape valve for the regime, preventing social pressures from exploding. In 1980, Castro also used it as a means of making room in prisons, and many common criminals were put on boats in Mariel who would later commit crimes in the U.S. By the early 1980s, Cubans in the U.S.— the emigrants and their children — exceeded one million.

The Cuban economy has continued to be plagued by worker absenteeism, inefficiency and low productivity, despite the limited introduction of material incentives. In addition to the basic economic model, several factors combined to further limit economic growth in the 1980s, prior to the collapse of communism in the Soviet Union and Eastern Europe. The Reagan administration reinvigorated the policy of economic isolation of Cuba, and continued to restrict Cuba's access to credit. In 1985, Hurricane Kate wreaked havoc on the sugar harvest; in 1986, the worst drought in a decade further reduced sugar production. The little sugar they did produced was worth even less on the international market. In 1980, a pound of sugar was worth 29 cents, but by 1985 this had declined to 4 cents. Declining oil prices in 1986 further reduced government revenues. Cuba and the Soviet Union had long exchanged sugar for oil at terms preferential to the Cubans, and the Cuban government would re-export a considerable amount of the oil that they had imported, thus generating much needed foreign exchange. Between 1983 and 1985, oil exports accounted for between 40 percent and 42 percent of Cuba's hard-currency earnings; in 1986 this dropped to 27 percent.

That was, however, only a taste of things to come. The collapse of the communist governments in Eastern Europe in 1989 and of the Soviet Union in 1991 gutted the Cuban economy and posed a severe challenge to the leadership. Since the early 1960s, 70 percent to 90 percent of Cuba's international trade had been with the former Soviet Union and the Eastern Bloc. The Soviets also supported Cuba through subsidies as well as bankrolling and often renegotiating the latter's trade deficit, which by 1985 had reached almost $30 billion. With the end of the Soviet Union and COMECON (the Community for Economic Cooperation), an important source of credit and oil was closed off and trade with Eastern Europe all but disappeared. Exports from the former Soviet bloc to Cuba plummeted by about 70 percent from 1989 to 1993, while the value of imports from all sources dropped from $8 billion to $1.7 billion. By 1993, Soviet oil shipments had fallen 90 percent, and fertilizers fell 80 percent from pre–1989 levels. Overall, between 1989 and 1993, Cuba's GDP contracted by at least 35 percent, at least half of the factories became inoperative, and shortages led to malnutrition, blackouts, despair and renewed efforts to flee the island by thousands of Cubans. The sugar crop, which had stood at 8.1 million tons in 1991, was cut almost in half by 1993, when the harvest yielded 4.2 million tons.

In an effort to climb out of economic ruin, the government began a concerted effort to develop the tourism and biotechnology sectors and to attract foreign investment from new sources. Canada, Spain, Italy, Japan,

Mexico and other countries expanded trade and investment projects with Cuba. As a result of investment and marketing, tourism grew significantly and consistently, and by the late 1990s more than 1.5 million tourists would visit the island annually. Presently, Cuba imports some $5 billion of goods annually, approximately $800 million of which is food products—cooking oil, rice, wheat, corn, soy, powered milk, and poultry. It is a testament to the resiliency of the repressive apparatus that the regime was able to survive near total economic collapse.

Things always seem to be changing in Cuba, but little actually changes. Prior to the revolution, Cuba was primarily a sugar producer; land was held as *latifundia*, or in large holdings; there was only a modicum of light industry, the economy was dependent on the U.S.; and there were significant levels of underemployment. Rather than "trading in" this situation for a new one, at this level the revolution changed little. Instead of relying on the United States, Cuba became a client state of the Soviet Union, even more dependent on sugar production, with little new industry and increased underemployment. To some extent this last characteristic reflects the improvements in education, although economic stagnation has clearly exacerbated the situation.

As we have seen, much of the history of Cuba is the history of a conflict between social and political monism and pluralism. The remainder of this work examines the ways monism is manifest in Cuba under the Castro regime, and how Cubans have responded to it.

CHAPTER 2

First Flight

I had read about Cuban history and was eager to see where many of the books left off. Thinking back on it, uncertainty and ambiguity have plagued my involvement in Cuba since the beginning. Would the department or treasury grant me a license to travel to Cuba, and if so, would the Cubans really give me a hotel room with this bible-page-thin voucher I had? And that was even before I saw the words "Cubana" fuzzily spray-painted on the side of an old Russian jetliner. Airborne, it was soon after the steward had handed out translucent ham and butter sandwiches for lunch that I saw the island for the first time. I remember looking from the window and thinking. "The forbidden isle." My eyes savored it from there until we reached Havana, soaking up the surfside, the greenery and the round plots of ground, all the while wondering why this place should be off limits to so many.

Having passed through customs, I was pleasantly surprised to find among the anxious, packed crowd a tour agent waiting to pick me up. Jostled and shoved, he struggled to hold in view a small card with my name spelled incorrectly. There was something odd about the twenty-some minute ride into Havana that took me a while to place. Soon I realized that there were almost no other vehicles, save for a few other cabs and some large eighteen-wheelers groaning along, some with passenger heads popping up from where the cargo should be. The open road proved irresistible to my driver and soon I found myself in an impromptu road race with another cab: two old beat-up Russian-made Ladas trying to out-wheeze each other.

The desolation of the streets was echoed in the lobby of the decaying Hotel Lincoln. The power was out, and the darkness accentuated the dank, damp, still lobby. Climbing six flights of stairs, I was shown to my threadbare room, which was without electricity or air conditioning. Deciding to see the town, I walked down the corridor and took the stairs down towards the lobby. Just before I got there, I found myself at a large iron door, locked, with protective spikes on top. I called out, and someone came to open it.

Venturing outside into the humid, embracing, blinding tropical heat, I soon found my way to the famous Malecón. This undulating seaside drive has become an archetypal symbol of Cuba, originally designed by Cubans and built under American engineers during the U.S. occupation of the country in the early 1900s. I had some fears about being on the streets. Given that Castro had been assuring everybody for the past several decades that gringos are imperialists, I was concerned that I would not be well received. This feeling was exacerbated by the countless whistles and shouts which enveloped me like a cloud on my walk. On two counts, I did not have to worry. One, everyone thought I was a German and two on the whole Cubans love Americans, and America. It came as both a shock and a relief that when someone approached me and said "Wie geht es Ihnen?" and I responded in Spanish that I was an American, he lit up with a broad smile and suddenly reached out to shake hands. Never in all of my travels in Latin America has anyone responded with such delight upon learning my nationality.

Soon, I was chatting with a small crowd. It was as if they had never seen an American, but it probably had as much to do with the fact that there did not appear to be much else to break up their routine. Unprompted, a group of Rastafarian musicians were very frank, to the point of profanity, in expressing their unhappiness in Cuba, one exclaiming, "This place is shit and it's all got to end!" I hadn't even been on the ground for two hours, and here I was chatting with a bunch of counterrevolutionaries. As it turned out, many of the people I spoke with were hungry and asked for food. In the space of an hour or so I lost count of how many people offered to sell me Cuban pesos, which foreigners cannot spend in Cuba; puros, or cigars, which I do not smoke; or steroids (stolen from some government laboratory), which I do not take. The number was sufficient to make me want to get a T-shirt printed up, saying in bold letters, "Ni Pesos, Ni Puros." I spoke with more people in an hour than I had spoken with in a month in Spain.

Feeling the heat, both atmospheric and social, I thought it was time to beat a retreat to the clammy recesses of my hotel room. Anyway, it was getting close to dinnertime. Later, coming down the stairs again, I found a crowd in the lobby, including many Cubans. Seeing me, a foreigner in their midst, a hotel employee ushered me into the air-conditioned restaurant. Here was "tourist apartheid" in action, where tourists are given preferential, often exclusive, access to everything, and the Cubans get to watch from the outside. It's interesting that this kind of practice was one of Castro's complaints before the revolution. Apparently he decided it wasn't such a bad policy after all.

In any case, as this was a low-end hotel, the policy was to let Cubans eat in the restaurant, if they could pay and no tourist would have to wait. So they gathered, and waited, while I surveyed the menu and listened to a group of musicians languidly strumming tunes which they had clearly played too many times before. Despite the listed items on the menu, it seemed that the evening's offering was pasta. At least they had cold beer for the long wait ahead. Those who work in the restaurants and other tourist facilities are what Lenin would call, in a capitalist context, the "labor aristocracy." They get to pilfer food and other luxury items like soap and shampoo from the hotels and other tourist places where they work. Two hours and a plate of cold pasta later, I went to my room to rest. The hungry, smoke-bathed crowd in the lobby had only grown in size and volume, and the restaurant was still mostly empty. They were waiting to pay for leftovers.

Waking up the next morning, I opened the shaky, peeling French windows of my room and was treated to a beautiful, sixth-floor view of the city: lovely in its tranquility graced with a morning haze, but grim in its filth, decay and permeating sense of despair. Many people were still asleep with their windows open, often shielded by an exterior Venetian-type blind propped out or slung over a railing. Peering towards the end of the bay, I saw the source of the morning haze: the oil refinery with its black smoke billowing towards the city. Descending for breakfast, I perused the menu, an exercise in what turned out to be a process of elimination. No eggs. No ham. No juice. A bologna sandwich? For breakfast? Sure. The bologna factory was apparently still working, its product arriving piled high and cut almost as thick as the bread it was served on. At least I could mask its flavor with a cup of thick, sweet Cuban coffee.

During the morning I had several meetings at the National Archive, where the people were quite interested in developing research projects with American colleagues. Later, walking back towards the hotel, I heard music nearby. Following it like a scent, I stumbled upon a block party. It was easy to have block parties in Havana, as there was no traffic to block and plenty of people otherwise milling about. This one was quite a lively affair, someone having found a source of electricity and rigged up some amplifiers. Electric guitars were playing, bottles of rum were being passed freely around, and there was plenty of dancing in the streets. I was made most welcome, confirmed by inviting gestures and a bottle being passed to me. What was most interesting, other than the fact that Cubans on the whole are extremely friendly, was one of the ladies who was dancing. At least in her sixties and jealously guarding her own bottle of rum, her dance was like an erotic religious procession of one. Slow swings of her hips and rhythmic shakes of her breasts were punctuated with fervent signs of the cross, imploring gazes to the heavens and seductive enticements to those in the crowd to join her. I was amazed at what religious repression, sexual deprivation and alcohol can produce.

Blending out more successfully than I had blended in, I decided to visit some of the historic sites. It seems that the number of people willing to serve as impromptu tour guides is directly proportional to the degree to which people in the streets are hungry or otherwise deprived. There were plenty of people eager to share the secrets of local history. Leaving an old fort, I was approached by two boys, no older than sixteen or seventeen, trying to look their best in their tattered clothes. They took the responsibility upon themselves to show me the town. We spent the day together, walking, talking, visiting museums and drinking colas. They made it clear how unhappy and fed up they were, how they had no opportunity, how they wanted to escape the island.

Interestingly, though, during a visit to the Museum of the Revolution, they stood in awe of a uniform Ché Guevara had worn decades ago. They hated their chains, but they respected those who had forged them. They are not alone. Later I would meet an elderly lady who fought in the revolution and just about goes crazy whenever the subject of Castro is brought up, frowning, cursing and storming out of the room. But when she sees him give a speech, she is moved to tears and seems to adore the man. The Beard, or "La Barba," does have a way with the Cubans. He is charismatic, and what people in the U.S. often don't understand is that to the Cubans, and many Latin Americans, he is a nationalist first and a communist second. And when charisma fails there is always the secret police.

One of my self-appointed tour guides explained to me that he worked in a slaughterhouse. He proceeded to explain in grim detail how the animals are herded, then channeled down a chute, and how his job is to dispatch them with an electric shock to the neck before they are drained of their blood and cut to pieces. I guess the cattle are the only ones in Cuba who long for a power outage. I remarked to him how depressing his job must be, but he disagreed: he not only ate copious amounts of fresh beef but also sold plenty of it on the black market. It was, apparently, a great job. Towards the end of our day together, my two new friends wanted to sell me their extensive LP record collection. I tried to explain to them that almost no one uses record players anymore, but they were not convinced. Instead, I wanted to give them a few dollars for having shown me around. Revealing a modest wad of cash, I had until then never seen people run away at the sight of greenbacks. It was as if they suddenly did not even know me. Were they so hard-core that they did not want to soil their hands with the virus of capitalism? I coaxed them back, and learned that if a Cuban (at that time) was caught with a single dollar bill, he would be imprisoned. In the end they took their chances, and the money, and made a quick exit.

Before too long, my time was up. Fortunately my cab fare back to the airport had already been paid for. I waited in the lobby to be picked up, and waited, and waited. The front desk staff was scrambling to find the cab that was scheduled to pick me up. Soon, they were looking for any cab. Desperate and almost certain I was going to miss my flight, I headed towards the Malecón. In the midday heat it was as deserted as a scene from "The Omega Man." Finally, a cab came barreling down the road, and I decided that a body block was my only chance. Bringing the vehicle to a halt right before my knees, I asked the driver to take me to the airport. With a good-natured smile, he complained that he was about to finish his shift. The promise of a nice tip persuaded him, and he turned around and off we went to the airport.

There was no line at the Cubana desk. The agent, officious and uniformed, refused to give me my boarding pass, telling me I was too late. I explained that the person who was paid to pick me up never did and that the hotel could not find a cab. He still refused. I explained that I had only carry-on luggage, that the plane had not even started to board yet and that I was out of cash. He went to speak to his boss, and then still refused. But then a curious thing happened. During this time, I had been holding my passport, and on top of it, my ticket. Placing my ticket on the counter, a subtle glance indicated that he notice my American passport, and he suddenly became quite helpful. He again spoke to his boss, and I was finally issued a boarding pass. They say a good sailor never questions a fair wind, and with a thank you I was on my way to customs.

The person who was collecting documents and checking passports mentioned what a nice watch I had. I thanked him, noting that it was a gift. As I was wondering if it was to be my ransom, he proudly pointed to his own, which was the identical model. Now we were comrades, and I was out of there. Upon arriving in Cancún, one thing grabbed my attention: newsstands. Lots of them, overflowing with papers and magazines. It hit me how Castro doesn't want anyone in Cuba to have information to form their own opinions, an attitude that also applies to the Cuban Right in the U.S.

CHAPTER 3

Living the Monistic Life

Like all Cubans, my friend Felipe lives in fear. He speaks English, Italian, German, Russian, and, of course, Spanish. He has a degree as a pharmacist, but the money is much better for him and his wife and two little boys as a tourist guide. Associating with foreigners— though that is his government-approved profession — puts him under suspicion. For that reason, whether or not he is on duty, he wears his tourist guide ID wherever he goes.

After the anti-government riots on the Malecón in 1994, Castro created a para-police force called the Boinas Negras, or black berets. It consists of young men, brought to Havana from the villages, who intimidate and rough up anyone they think is counter-revolutionary or otherwise breaking the most minor of laws. Highly indoctrinated and lacking any real connection to the Habaneros, they are much less likely to be "corrupted" by personal relations with them. Once I was in the crafts market near the Malecón, looking to add to my collection of old cigar labels. Suddenly two trucks, with about thirty or so black berets in the back of each, came to a halt at two corners bordering the market. Many locals started to walk away rapidly, clearly hoping to not be stopped.

The black berets fanned out and began to stop people, checking identifications, license plates, asking where they work, where they were going. A little girl was beating on a pot with a spoon, but her mother snatched the spoon away from her and both slipped out of sight into a doorway. Later I was told that, with few exceptions, those found to be doing something they should not, or not doing something they should, or just somehow looking wrong, are put into the military trucks and taken away for more questioning and general harassment. The fact that the black berets have carte blanche irritates even the local Havana police, but, like all Cubans, they know better than to challenge their power.

Felipe avoids the neighborhoods where the black berets are deployed on any given day. He especially fears the consequences of spending too much time with me. I cannot help assuming that he reports, at least minimally, to the neighborhood Committee for the Defense of the Revolution, but still I think he is like many in Cuba: doing the minimum for the government and hoping to get by until the big change comes.

One day his fear turned to dread. Felipe had recently moved to a new apartment in Vedado, a central Havana neighborhood closer than his previous one to the hotels where many of his tourist clients stay. Like most living quarters in Havana, it was small, cramped, and neighbors could easily hear what you had to say, especially if you raised your voice. Like most Cubans, and Americans for that matter, Felipe had heard as much as he could stand of Elián Gonzalez, the Cuban nine-year-old who in 2000 was the center of a tug-of-war between the Castro government and the Miami Cubans. Every afternoon for hours, the two television stations showed the same roundtable talk about the latest developments in the case, how it was emblematic of the relationship between the two countries, and how it showed everything that was wrong with the U.S. One day, wanting to drown out the incessant arguing of his neighbors, he turned on the television, only to be yet again greeted by the same broken record on both channels. He blurted out to his wife, "I tell you what they should do with that damn kid. Tell the Americans to take him out to sea and drop him where they found him, and let the Cuban navy come and get him."

He didn't think much about his rather creative contribution to resolving the crisis until the next day. Returning from taking a group of Canadian tourists to Ernest Hemingway's well-preserved home on the outskirts of Havana, he found his wife quiet, her eyes dark with worry. She told him that he had a message that the head of the building's Committee for the Defense of the Revolution, or CDR, wanted to meet with him the next day. The CDRs are usually block-level organizations whose job it is to detect, prevent and report counter-revolutionary activity. It seemed that his neighbors had stopped quarreling long enough to hear him and had reported his outburst. Seized by panic, he went down the three flights of stairs to take a hasty walk around the neighborhood. Later, he could not sleep, he could not eat, and he certainly could not think of a good excuse for what he had said. The following morning, knowing he could not wait any longer because the dread was eating him alive, he decided he had to get it over with.

Felipe knocked politely at the door of the first floor apartment of the building's thought cop, having decided to turn himself in. He entered contritely while at the same time trying to act as if he did not know why he had been called. The boss told him that he had been keeping an eye on him, and had also asked Felipe's neighbors to do the same. Tears welled up. He was about to beg for forgiveness. The boss let his comments sink in, and then added that he himself had also been doing some checking up on him. Now the stress peppered Felipe's vision with spots of light. His thoughts racing, he figured if he was lucky he might only lose his job, go to jail. He could send his wife back to Cienfuegos, where she had family, who could help raise their two little boys.

After another pause, the boss said that he had given a lot of thought to the information that he had gathered, and for that reason wanted to offer Felipe the post of CDR captain for his floor. Felipe now grew dizzy with relief but was able to compose himself, hoping his sweat had not betrayed him and that the tears welling in his eyes would be interpreted as signs of gratitude and joy. Felipe told the boss how honored he was at the nomination, how he had long wished to serve the revolution in that way. But, he added, he worked as a tour guide and kept long and irregular hours, which would interfere with his ability to keep the proper vigilance over the other residents in the building. Besides, as a tour guide, his primary responsibility was to educate foreigners about the revolution. Despite his desire to do both, he just did not see how he could both defend the revolution at home and export it at the same time. He hoped that the boss would understand, which he did.

Just as sad as his fear of the CDR boss is Felipe's fear of dreaming — not in terms of nightmares, but in terms of having hopes, a vision to direct his life. One day over lunch we were talking about crazy ideas. My argument was that most great ideas start out as crazy ideas, that ideas generally accepted as truth often started their journey as heresy. If it has worth, the persecuted idea is slowly accepted by a minority, and, gaining more steam, ultimately by a great many. As a result, people should dream, should be encouraged to have "crazy" ideas. Such a creative process, subjected to the marketplace of ideas, is at the root of much human progress. Crazy ideas have also created much misery, as a visit to Cuba will amply demonstrate. But in Cuba and elsewhere this usually happens when ideas are offered to the exclusion of others without being tested by debate.

Deep into this conversation, Felipe, his brow furrowed and looking perplexed, told me, "Nick, all this talk is crazy!" To which I responded that that was perhaps so, but he was crazy not to dream, that without dreams, without crazy ideas, where was he going? "But Nick, don't you see that dreaming is one thing, trying to live it is another? If someone here is going to realize a dream he will probably have to break the law, and end up in jail, or raft to Miami."

We sat silent for a moment. Twirling his spaghetti slowly on his spoon and looking concerned, Felipe said, "Nick, you need a protector. You know that in my religion we all have guardians, and I now know that yours is Chango, the orisha [god] of fire, lightning and war." In Santería, the Cuban folk religion brought over from Africa with the slaves and somewhat fused with Catholicism, individuals at some point learn that one of its deities is their guardian spirit. Each orisha is also represented by colored beads arranged in a distinct pattern. The next day, Felipe gave me a necklace of Santería beads, which he told me his mother had given to him, and which was a rare honor to give and receive. Respectfully, I wore them. Over the following days, they attracted a lot of attention on the street. I would be walking, and in the manner of a salute, people would say, "Chango," as they passed.

Fear is perhaps the easiest emotion to read in someone's eyes, and it has been the handmaiden of many Cuban rulers. Once, I had decided to try the famous Coppelia ice cream at their one square block complex in central Havana. The line, for once, was not all the way to the street, and upon entering the restaurant, not knowing there was a separate section for foreigners, I took a seat among the Cubans. A girl of about eighteen came and took my order, and before too long I was savoring a generous portion of chocolate ice cream and cake. It would have been nothing out of the ordinary, except for the fact that at first there was one policeman watching me, and about five minutes later word had spread and there were several police around me, all watching me eat. I ate slowly, giving thought to the spectators, letting them fully witness each melting spoonful.

Until then, I had never realized that the consumption of ice cream was a national security issue. My waitress also saw what was going on, though she continued to run madly to and fro, bringing people their orders, and casting furtive glances towards the police, and at me. She was terrified: she had served a foreigner in the part that only took Cuban people and pesos, and she had told me that it was OK to pay in dollars. Finishing my helping and beginning to realize the situation, I flagged her down to pay. We were both in a bind. I had no Cuban pesos, as they are not accepted from nor generally given to foreigners in Cuba, and there was this small crowd of policemen watching everything. In the end, I slipped some money under my plate as discreetly as possible, and left. I will never forget the fear in her chestnut eyes, dark, deep, and knowing that she would at best be fired, at worst sent to jail. And all for a plate of ice cream and cake.

It is said that people get the governments they deserve. I disagree; the Cuban people deserve a whole lot better. Who can blame them if they don't want to be beaten, jailed, or shot? The fact is that repression works.

Here you have a small group of people who, through intimidation, threats, and the arbitrary exercise of power mixed with a dose of nationalist charisma, manage to keep eleven million people down. Many times I would ask Felipe how the situation was, and he would invariably tell me that the government, and the people, were more nervous and on edge, and that the repression had only increased since my last visit. There is little, if any, social trust. It is a communist dictatorship, but it is better called a despotism or tyranny decorated with Marxist rhetoric and presented in the tradition of the Latin American *caudillo*, or strongman — a legacy of Spanish colonial rule.

This absence of trust permeates even the highest levels. On a visit to New Orleans to give a talk, the Cuban Chief of Mission, who likes to be called "Ambassador," came with an aide. The aide was partly no doubt to protect him, but also served to keep an eye on him. By traveling in twos they keep an eye on each other to better ensure that they do what they are supposed to. The "ambassador" offered the standard talk condemning the embargo; the Cuban American Right was out in force, mocking, heckling, making speeches and walking out. The two Cubans stood together, bound by, among other things, their mutual threat of blackmail. The Right did rattle their cage a bit, as was obvious by the way they walked quickly to the car afterwards, glancing over their shoulders several times.

In Cuba, the secret police and especially their agents are nearly everywhere. Marcus Wolf, the former head of East Germany's *stasi*, describes in his memoirs how he set up the Cuban Intelligence Service on the pattern of his own secret service. There are many uniformed police around, but many more are dressed as civilians, and even more are neighbors, relatives, and even "friends" who have become reluctantly entangled in that cruel system. In Cuba, the already mentioned Committees for the Defense of the Revolution are especially important. The system is subtle. The security forces do not break down your door at midnight and haul you away, Argentine fashion. Instead they watch you, and when you err, they try to persuade you to mend your ways. If that does not work they threaten you, or organize some neighbors, co-workers or even a mob to terrorize or even beat you, and if that does not work, then they put you in jail.

The irony is that such a system could implant itself in Cuba. On the whole, Cubans are the most direct, in-your-face people I have known anywhere. They do not do a good job of hiding their feelings, and they are not shy. They answer the phone shouting, "I'm listening!" and the conversation then often increases in volume. It takes a bit of getting used to, but if someone is shouting in your face and gesticulating aggressively, they are simply expressing themselves, no offense intended. Keeping the Cubans down cannot be as easy as it looks to the casual observer. But then again, it's always the sign of a professional to make something difficult look easy.

Scarcity and fear define the lives of most Cubans. Scarcity of everything except fear, and of course there is no scarcity of long lines. Scarcity drives people to do all kinds of things that they would not otherwise do. The invisible glue holding the entire thing together is fear. The beauty of fear is that it is silent, deep, constant, and at once general and very individual. Fear is like a chain, holding you back from doing what you want to, gnawing all the time. Even those who follow the rules and believe in the system are not immune to fear, though they may feel somewhat more insulated by being its agent. When a vague boundary has been crossed, fear transforms itself into its even worse cousin, dread. Dread is the worst, because like fear, it is constant, but like a gun pointed at you, you never know when it will go off. Dread is the fear of actually experiencing one's fears, of a date with what you have been trying so hard to avoid. Fear and dread are what allow the system to continue in the midst of scarcity. Taxi drivers and shoe shiners are always good gauges of local opinion. There are not many shoe shiners in Havana, but one, near the Sevilla Hotel at the edge of the beautiful Old Town, told me, "I have never seen things this bad." He was 87, born in 1913.

Everyone, including government officials, must, however, find something to eat in this nation of foragers, and even the purveyors of fear contend with scarcity. Once, I was wrapping up a meeting with a man I know who served in Cuba's intelligence services in Europe for many years. The intelligence folks are usually more open than others, perhaps because they are the source of fear, they have less of it. Also, they may criticize the regime to encourage the person they are talking to expose their own views. After having coffee and trying to find out who was trying to scuttle my projects, I mentioned that I was headed to another meeting on the other side of town. He offered to drive me, no doubt to see where I was going, and I accepted. On the way, he complained, more despairingly than usual, about how little money he has, how his children eat like wolves, how it will take thirty years at the present rate just to get where they were ten years ago, and so on. Between them, he and his wife, they earned twenty dollars a month, not bad for Cuba.

I know his income was actually a bit higher than this, as he got a couple of hundred from friends across the straits, selling that most sought after product, information. One must be careful not to think that he did not also report the contacts, if not the earnings, to his own people, and anyway his products may have been defective "seconds." On the way across town, as the windshield wipers slowly smudged the rain on the windshield,

I offered to fill up his car with gas, since it was a bit of a drive. This he declined, telling me he would do it later as there was a free market place he went to and got a good rate. In any case, pleased that he had helped me to locate the source of my problem and wanting to maintain good relations, compromised though they were by his divided loyalties, I casually slipped a twenty in the book he had been reading. Not a word was spoken, nor the act concealed. It was never clear to me if he wanted to turn American informer, thinking me an intelligence agent; if he was trying to compromise me, or if he simply wanted the money. Perhaps all were true.

Scarcity is the common denominator of Cuba. Go into one of the (non-tourist) government stores, and you will see a grimly lit, almost empty warehouse with some notes chalked on a board: a long list saying what they do not have, and a very short one listing what is available. Even if there were products to buy with the ration card that Cubans are given, it would not be enough. The same is true of their wages. People earn between eight and sixteen dollars a month. A very lucky doctor might make twenty. Their wages are paid in pesos, which are effectively non-convertible and made even less valuable by the fact that much of the economy has become dollarized. The paper currency, because it has been circulating far longer than it would in most places, is limp with a smooth sheen of ingrained filth. Because Cubans earn so little, they must turn to the black (or, as some call it, "free") market. There is also a lively barter economy, exchanging products or services. There is no other way. A one-dollar tip will get you far in Cuba, a five dollar one just about anything.

Unless you have dollars, there is very little in the way of even small luxuries. The hotels and government elite are provided for first and what is left goes to the ordinary Cubans. There is a safety net over poverty in Cuba, but it is very close to the ground. The scarcity of public transportation, the lack of junk food (one of Cuba's good points), and the necessity of a largely vegetarian diet means that there are very few obese people in Cuba. The Cuban government has focused on preventative care, and in that regard they have made advances which some other countries would do well to look at. They have trained thousands of doctors and have improved the health of the population, and focused a lot of resources on rural areas.

The argument, however, that the embargo kills people by preventing Cuba from obtaining pharmaceuticals doesn't hold water. Almost any drug in the world can be bought, and bought relatively cheaply, in developing countries. And for a few years now, Cuba has been able to purchase drugs directly from the United States, though it is a cumbersome process. The real problem is that the economy is a wreck, and yet again the embargo is used as a fig leaf in an attempt to conceal the shortcomings of the Cuban government. Still, if you are going to get sick, Cuba is a good place to do so. If you are in the cab coming in from the airport and have a cardiac arrest, don't despair; your cab driver is probably an M.D. Should you happen to trip on the stairs going into your hotel, no problem; the doorman is probably a physician as well. Medical care is widely available in Cuba, though not in the way envisioned by the leadership, or by physicians for that matter.

People who laud the Cuban example for health and educational systems would do well to take a trip to Costa Rica. There, they have achieved very similar indices in health and education, and there is a much more equitable distribution of wealth than in other Latin American countries. Not to say that they, like Cuba, don't have their problems, but they have a political system that allows people to express their opinions and to choose their rulers and an economic and educational system that provides opportunities.

In Cuba, the only way to do a little better than the rest is either to get a lucrative black-market racket going, such as selling cigars stolen from the factories, or to get a job in the tourist sector. The latter is the place to be, because even though you are earning less than you would in the black-market cigar industry, you do not risk jail time while making your living. Also, you can get some of the benefits of the black market by hooking people up, brokering things, etc. It's not so much that the wages are higher there, but that the tips are higher than the wages. For example, the doorman at my favorite hotel, a chivalrous, energetic and engaging man, makes just under six dollars a month. I nearly double his income every time I arrive with a five-dollar tip. The problem is that while there are a lot of tourists, they are of the notoriously stingy variety. Few high rollers come to Cuba these days. Still, another advantage of working in the tourist economy is that, at least in hotels and restaurants, you can get a square meal, and in the case of hotels, get to squirrel away soap, shampoo and other things for which there is a family need and a wider market.

A sad byproduct of scarcity combined with tourism is prostitution. I grew up in New Orleans, the City of Sin, but it pales in comparison to the Pearl of the Caribbean. Prostitution is not only a legal profession in Cuba, within certain limits, but also a legitimate one. The spin is that these women are not really prostitutes, or *jinateras*, but just dates, and their clear objective is to get married and get out. Naturally, their dates take good care of them, and they come home with lots of money. If there is sex, it is simply "incidental." And some actually do get married, evidenced by the brisk bookings in the Wedding Palace and related visa petitions in the Italian, German and Spanish embassies. Many are also educated, trained business professionals who bring new meaning to the phrase "the double day." Others are children still in their teens, without a lot of expand in their spandex. Often coming in from the provinces, they are found all over, especially cruising the Malecón, and tourist locations, and walking hand in hand with their tricks in hotels, restaurants, bars and discos. Holding hands is key, because unless they are physically attached to their "date," they will be refused admittance, they are Cubans after all. With Castro as its host, Fantasy Island does have its appeal, but when you see so many fat, unshaven elderly men consorting with girls the age of their granddaughters, it gets a little unseemly.

Combine the social legitimacy of prostitution with the assertive, forward nature of many Cubans, and watch out! The women know what they have and want everyone else to know as well. There is probably more spandex sold there per capita than anywhere else in the world. One afternoon I was walking down the Malecón, and I noticed that about twenty feet ahead of me four *jinateras* were joining to form a spandex wall that I would have to go either through or around. They were as unwilling to let me pass as I was unwilling to detour, and I was greeted first by their entreaties, and later their protests, as I opened a path and continued on my way. Another time, at night, I was showing four university deans around and perhaps six ladies formed a gantlet around us, enticing us with their vivid suggestions and demonstrating just how good a massage could be.

They do not like to take no for an answer, and act hurt, reminding you that you have only seen part of Cuba unless you have spent an evening with them. One need not always go on the streets for this. In some restaurants it is easier to get a prostitute than a waiter, and some do manage to filter into the hotels. In one hotel I stayed at there was a sweet, attractive woman who was the housekeeper. Coming into the lobby one Saturday evening, I saw her dressed in good-looking street clothes instead of her powder blue striped uniform. I told her how nice she looked, and she gave a most suggestive smile, telling me how nice I also looked that evening. It was only as the elevator door closed that I realized that, no, she wasn't the housekeeper after all. Perhaps her sister.

After a late dinner at a *paladar*—a small private restaurant in people's homes—a gay friend of mine and I headed back to our hotel along the Malecón around midnight. There were hundreds of people out enjoying the sticky, salty night breeze. Suddenly, out of nowhere, a huge black woman leaped from the seawall, wrapping her arms around my short friend, swallowing him in her breasts. Possessed with both passion and glee, she had found her man, screaming, "He's mine, he's mine!" Rushing to his rescue, I said firmly, "No, he's mine," and only with the greatest reluctance did she free him from her grasp and allow him to breathe again. Finally arriving at the Habana Libre Hotel, I remembered it was Saturday night, and the disco on the top floor would be in full swing. Outside, it was as if they were expecting Julio Iglesias but had neglected to provide crowd control. Girls in their teens, and younger, were dressed, or rather undressed, for the evening, hoping to find a date who would hold their hand, pay their cover and spend the evening with them. I now know how rock stars feel when they arrive at the show, and how hard it is to get past pawing, pleading, imploring girls without an escort. No night on the town could ever compare to what Havana has to offer. The sad thing is what is being offered.

It is ironic that prostitution should flourish where there has been some progress in eroding machismo culture. It's not that there is a short-age of whistling, or of beautiful women to whistle at, but overall it is not as extreme as, say, in Mexico. What is interesting is how this has been done. Usually it is asserted that women achieve their independence through having an independent income. This Marx would have predicted, the eco-nomic driving the social. And in the case of prostitution in Cuba it has been the case. But otherwise you do not achieve economic independence there by being formally employed, because you cannot survive on a state salary. Also, even if you have economic independence, you may not be able to exercise it by, for example, getting your own place to live. Many divorced couples still live together because of a lack of housing alterna-tives. The way machismo has been eroded is through legislation. Laws that mandate such things as that men must equally share in the housework, even if unenforceable, have helped to create a different climate. Divorce, for what it is worth if you are still living with your ex, is also easier. This reflects the erosion of the influence of the Catholic Church, not that it was ever as powerful in Cuba as in other Latin American countries. It is indeed strange that although people are rarely allowed to sell their products in an open market in Cuba, women can sell their bodies quite openly.

Among Cubans, there is a tolerance of homosexuality and inter-racial relationships that you don't see in other countries. Now more than ever, Cuba is basically a black country. Many of the whites left early on, leav-ing varying shades of black and brown to experience Castro's economic policies. Racism certainly still exists, and there aren't a whole lot of blacks or mulattos in the higher positions of government. As a result, and per-haps also from somewhat hypocritical calls by Castro to abandon racism, you do see many more mixed couples there than in the States. Likewise, homosexuality is more open there, though by no means as open as in some parts of the U.S. This Castro has in the past tried to suppress, at one point sending gays, or those accused as such, to special camps where they could expiate their perceived errors through hard labor. It just didn't work. I don't know why homosexuality is more open in Cuba, but it may be partly that the deeply repressive nature of the system causes people to express themselves in other ways.

Castro believes in the pendulum theory of control: let things go pretty far one way, then throw it back the other way for a while, and so on. Look at the history of farmer's markets under Castro, *paladars* and other minimal or pseudo liberalizing programs, and you will see that the pendulum always swings the other way. People are kept off balance, never knowing when they will wake up to find that the rules have changed, and they are suddenly doing something wrong. There is no predictability or expectation of fair play. What had yesterday been legal and condoned is today condemned as anti-revolutionary and punishable by fines and jail. By the late '90s, the pendulum had swung one way, a long way, in the sex-tourism industry; so far, in fact, that it was clear that eventually it would have to swing the other way. To play with that industry is to play with the national economy. It was an especially fine line to walk, because so, very many people came to the Bangkok of the Caribbean to have sex with women and girls. The country depended on it; the entire economy had been reconfigured away from sugar towards tourism. Instead of "a chicken in every pot," it was "free porno in every hotel room."

I asked a lot of people who work in the tourist industry to estimate what percent of unaccompanied male tourists come for sex. The answers I got ranged from eighty to ninety-five percent. Paulo, who plays a guitar in a band, asserted that those who don't come for sex the first time come back for it. Add to that good rum and Cuban cigars and you have a very volatile mix indeed. The problem was that too many people were having too much fun, and crime started to rise. Castro had his finger on the pulse, and when, one night in the late 90s a couple of arriving European tourists did not make it to their hotel room, but instead were taken out of town, robbed, and shot, he decided it was time to push the pendulum the other way.

Overnight, discos were closed and the streets were deserted, not only by jinateras but by everyone else it seemed. Young German men walked aimlessly, crestfallen, as if the world had ended, seeking the comfort that was no longer available. The only consolation was that the cable porn continued. Word travels fast, and the returning tourists, instead of telling tales of conquest, complained about how they were ripped off. Arriving one moist night, I asked a cab driver how the tourist economy was doing. To my surprise he said that since word had spread of the crackdown, the numbers of tourists had declined. The pendulum would swing the other way before too long, however. Castro had made his point, and he wasn't going to jeopardize the economy over it. Things may not be quite the way they were before, but soon people were again getting what they came for. The chief pimp had re-opened the brothel for business, once even publicly bragging about the quality of his whores.

What do Cubans who are not involved in the sex trade say about this? They do not like it, but understand all too well what drives people to sell their bodies. Sometimes they assume an air of distant sophistication; more often they feel degraded. One evening Amaury — the thirty-something cigar factory manager who had shown me his father's shrine to America — and I were driving down Quinta Avenida in the Miramar section for some drinks. Ahead we noticed some adolescent jinateras flagging us, and everyone else, down as if our cab was late to collect them. Amaury sighed, and remarked "Nick, my father told me how it was under Batista. Fidel says we changed it for good, but now look at it."

Everywhere the Communist Youth and other organizations paint their slogans in public venues, reminding people that it is all about "Fatherland or Death," or paint pictures of Ché Guevara with the ironic caption "We will always win." One, that I saw heading west out of town, reminded people that "You owe the Fatherland everything, the Fatherland owes you nothing," while another offered a picture of José Martí, the Cuban national hero, insisting that "Life is Duty." The saddest ones I saw read, "Real Human Rights are in Cuba," and, referring to the U.S., "They can take away everything but hope."

The irony of billboards is complemented by mass demonstrations. Castro can get the masses on the streets. It's easy: tell them through their workplaces and neighborhood CDRs to be on the Malecón at the prescribed hour. If you live farther out, transportation is provided. It is quite a logistical accomplishment, with trucks and buses bringing people in for hours. If they are not there it suggests counterrevolutionary tendencies. And just to make sure no one shows up and then drifts away, the entire length of the march is cordoned off with barricades manned by police, several to a block, sort of a reverse crowd control. I have seen them turn away dozens of marchers trying to go home early, directing them on to the end, the only exit. The end these days in Havana is the new "José Martí Anti-Imperialist Tribunal," commonly referred to as the "Protestodrome," located in front of the U.S. Mission. No doubt it will one day be a great venue for outdoor concerts, though it was built in less than two months at a cost of over two million dollars to rally the masses for the return of

Elián Gonzalez. At its head is a statue of Martí, holding a child, and pointing reproachfully at the mission. (The locals suggest that he is in fact telling the child where to apply for an exit visa.*) At the end of the long march and many speeches, Castro gives them a soft drink before sending them home.

The textbooks reinforce the view of Cuba's victimization at the hands of the United States. Spain and the Soviet Union are largely excluded from public criticism despite Castro's well-known feeling of being ignored in the Missile Crisis. On the private level, comments are different. Amaury, whose cousin fought in the proxy war in Angola, said, "The Americans may have given us a screwing, but they never sent us to fight their wars." Other than some lingering resentment, the Russians left hardly a trace in Cuba beyond their trademark ugly buildings and all but useless cars, the Lada and the Moscovich. Many Cubans refer to the Lada as a "Lata" which is the word for a tin can. Russia has no cultural affinity to Cuba, the way American culture does, and while they no doubt liked the climate, they couldn't act the part. Most of what they left behind is fodder for jokes. Clothes that are hopelessly out of style are referred to as "Russian fashion," and painfully slow and awkward conversations are said to be like a Russian movie. The Russians have, however, left some unexpected tools to aid in raising children. A very effective way to correct young miscreants is to tell them that if they don't behave they will be forced to watch Russian cartoons.

The Cuban educational system has certainly brought literacy to the vast majority of the population. It has also produced a great number of physicians, engineers and other technically skilled people. But one must ask, What is the good of learning to read if you cannot choose what you read? The real purpose of education is not to transfer information and have it repeated back to you, but rather to instill a critical and creative ability in people — to lead them to question and to challenge themselves and their society, to think of better ways to do things. This, however, is not among the goals of the Cuban educational system. Once I was seated in the prado, the tree lined walkway at the border of Old Havana, when a schoolgirl of about eight sat down next to me and we started to chat. I did not tell her that I was American, though of course she could tell by my accent that I was not a Cuban. I asked her what her favorite subjects were. Art was number one, mostly because she liked the teacher, but she said that she also liked Cuban history. I replied that that was good, everyone should study their country's history. I asked what they taught her about

---

**Thanks to Andrew Cawthorne for this information about the Tribunal.*

the U.S. Without a moment's hesitation, and with an innocence that could get her (or her family) in trouble, she replied, "Lies."

Fear and scarcity have a byproduct: conflict. Part of it has to do with Cuban culture, which seems prone to conflict. I found it notable that, when I was developing Tulane's Cuba program and asked Cubans I was working with what types of projects they wanted to develop, a disproportionate number had conflict resolution at or near the top of their lists. I tried on numerous occasions to offer short courses in Cuba on conflict resolution, but each time I was blocked by powers well above those I was working with. Perhaps the Cuban government does not just tolerate conflict, but, like drug pushers and their clientele, they need it. They need the Cubans at each other's throats. As long as people have an ax to grind they will keep turning each other in for alleged counter-revolutionary behavior, keeping stoked the fires of fear and dread. Just as importantly, they need the U.S. and Cuba to be at each other's throats: blaming outsiders is the time-tested way to cover up your own incompetence, and to keep people united by a sense of threat. The embargo is perfect for this, for it is an all-encompassing excuse for why things don't work. The official history reads that before 1959, all their problems came from their relations with the U.S.; now all their problems come from *not* having relations with the U.S. It is Castro who needs the embargo, not the U.S.; otherwise he would have to find a new enemy. It's not that all of the people are fooled, but some of them are.

It is strange how the situation can not only pit friend against friend, but brother against brother, even when they share the same desire. One sweltering, still afternoon Felipe returned home after spending a frustrating day with a group of Italians, half of whom wanted to visit historic sites and the other half to drink *mojitos*, the Cuban mint julep. Entering the apartment and finding his mother alone and quietly weeping, he knew things had just gotten worse. Pulling up a chair, he sat down and put his arm around her. She blurted out that his younger brother, Rodrigo, had earlier told her that he and three friends had for the past several weeks been gathering the pieces for and building a raft to "escape to America." Inwardly, Felipe, drawn in different directions by the thought of his wife and two little boys, felt a quiet urge to join them. His mother brought up another concern. It was not just that she would miss her youngest son; the middle one had already left after winning the visa lottery. That she could deal with, knowing that both would have a better future. What pained her most was the fear that Rodrigo would not even make it to the Florida shores.

Everyone knows that it is a dangerous trip, some estimates put the fatality rate at 50 percent. But the message had really hit home the week before when she heard that the son of one of her friends had been lost on the same crossing. The boy, whom she had known since he was born, and the six people with him had presumably been lost at sea, dehydrated, drowned or consumed by sharks. Her friend had called an elderly aunt in Miami three weeks previously to alert them that he would be coming. The weeks had passed in a silent suspense that progressively turned to anguish when he never showed up. Their story was not at all unusual. Rodrigo knew two of those who had been lost, but his determination pushed aside his doubts, and he had continued to build the raft.

When Rodrigo revealed the plan to his mother, she broke down. She pleaded with him to abandon the plan, reminding him of those who died, asking how it must feel to die of thirst, pleading with him to remember that such a death is often preceded by saltwater-induced insanity. Seeing that this had no effect on him she assured him that things would get better here, and in the meantime he might get lucky like his other brother and win a visa. This had even less effect; Rodrigo simply said that his life and his future were his own, and that he was not going to put his life on hold waiting for the Beard to die. Her pleas turned to angry demands, and the whole scene ended with him storming out of the apartment without even saying goodbye.

Felipe had arrived about forty minutes later, and, while shaken to see his mother in such a state, he was not surprised by the story. Rodrigo had clearly hinted about his plans last week, saying that he had decided to give himself his own exit visa, the hell if he was going to wait for the Beard or on Uncle Sam's visa-wheel of fortune. But now Felipe was drawn into the affair, as his mother demanded that he stop Rodrigo from going, by force if necessary. Felipe tried to get out of it, saying he had no idea where Rodrigo was building the raft, and even if he did Rodrigo's friends would surely defend him and he would be outnumbered. This only inflamed her agony, her tears gently eroded his resistance, and several minutes later he said he would do his best to stop him.

Heading out into the afternoon sun, Felipe had a pretty good idea where to find his brother. Rodrigo's best friend lived near the Malecón and had a large room off the second patio which had previously only been used for storage. A perfect place to build a raft. He went there, and, his knocking on the door ignored, began to clamor for Rodrigo, demanding that he open the door. After several minutes of banging and shouting, the door cracked open, and Felipe forced his way through. Rodrigo's usual joviality was replaced by a cold, distant look; he knew the nature of Felipe's errand. Felipe related his meeting with his mother, how broken she was, how by going he would kill her, how he would never forgive him, how Rodrigo should wait the whole thing out, how he would be eaten by sharks, reminding him what a weak swimmer he was. Rodrigo knew Felipe would surely leave himself if it were not for his children, and only taunted him, telling him that he should be man enough to make his own destiny, and that he was an idiot to stay, that he had always been a mama's boy anyway.

Felipe's heart was not in it, but his muscle was. The last comment set him off, and in a flash his fist connected with Rodrigo's jaw, sending him reeling and slamming into the wall, dislodging a slab of stucco. Rodrigo recovered and lunged headfirst, grabbing Felipe at the waist, trying to bring him down. Rodrigo's friends were bewildered by all of this, as Felipe had on many occasions made no secret of his own desire to leave. When he first entered the room they thought that he was going to ask if he could come along. What was certain was that Felipe was not only strong, but knew how to fight. While together they could have overpowered him, none wanted to pay the price. Also, it was a family dispute. So, as Rodrigo wrestled and called for help, they stood there, and in few a more seconds Felipe had Rodrigo pinned down, now bleeding from another blow, this one to the nose. As they both gasped for breath, Felipe demanded that he not go, and Rodrigo refused. Choking under the increasing pressure from Felipe's sizable forearm, he finally relented. Felipe made him promise not to him, but in his mother's name, before letting him go. Bloodied, beaten and humiliated, Rodrigo crouched in a corner, quietly weeping. Felipe, feeling the guilt of a traitor, warily eyed Rodrigo's friends, lest they go for him. Seeing his brother's blood on his one good "business" shirt, he walked over and helped Rodrigo up, and together they walked home.

CHAPTER 4

Love, Hate, and Chains

It must be difficult to live in a country you love but under a political system that you hate. The Cubans deal with their mixed emotions by splitting them. On the one hand, they turn the hatred they feel toward their chains onto other Cubans, especially those who help to maintain those chains. On the other hand, they idealize two seemingly antagonistic groups: those who have made their chains (Castro, Ché Guevara, and other founders of the revolution) and those who, who for various reasons, want to break their chains, specifically the Americans.

Rodrigo's thwarted effort to raft to the U.S. is emblematic of this ambivalence. Felipe and his mother intensely dislike the regime, but they in effect acted as its servants. Here, the family bonds survived the conflict, but Rodrigo will always wonder what his future would have been if he had succeeded in reaching America. He will probably always have some resentment toward his mother and brother. It is a lost opportunity that he will be reminded of constantly. Fleeing to America is such a common topic of conversation that it has even developed its own vocabulary. The verb "to raft" (*balsear* in Spanish) has become common. "He is going to raft, "We might as well raft," "It's time to raft" are not uncommon phrases among Cubans, especially the young.

The conflict in Felipe's family is typical because it is an example of self-policing. Policing by others is equally common. Celia, a woman who is very active though well into her seventies, had mentioned that she had been thinking of setting up a *batido*, or smoothie, stand outside her house. All she needed was a blender. She had the glasses, extension cord, and with her savings and a little help from her son Eduardo, a physician, she could buy the fruit and milk from the farmer's market. After that the profit would keep her going. Thinking it was a great idea, and wanting to help out someone I am fond of, the next day Eduardo and I "bank-rolled" her by buying her an Oster blender from one of the dollar shops.

The next day she was set up, a little table and stool in her doorway, the pitched, whining hum of the blender preparing custom-made *batidos*, mango, banana, papaya, for passersby. Within a few days, word of her cool, refreshing concoctions had spread. The sound of her loyal blender grinding ice in the alcove also served to attract clients, making for a brisk business. For two days, she was filled with glee, her excitement clearly showing in her raspy voice. Unfortunately, her burgeoning fame and success were a double-edged sword. The sound of the blender attracted not only customers, but also the attention of the police. Under threat of a large fine, she was forced to close down her stand after only two days of business. She was lucky that she got off with a warning that any other activities "of that sort" would bring stronger penalties.

It was not as if Celia had not otherwise played by the rules, even if she hated them. In fact, in her younger days, she had in a way helped make them as a young *guerrillera* working in the Havana underground. Despite losing faith in the intervening decades, she attended the CDR meetings where she listened respectfully and said the "right" things. Apart from her entrepreneurial foray, she kept a low profile. She even fulfilled that pointless and onerous task of CDR members, the neighborhood patrol. One night every two weeks, she and her youngest daughter patrolled a three-block area. No doubt the neighborhood slept soundly. Imagine a seventy-five-year-old woman and her daughter with Down syndrome, both armed with broomsticks, defending the revolution.

If there is so much hostility toward the government, why is there so much cooperation with it? Was it necessary for some of those who saw Celia's business to turn her in? Was it necessary to crack down on her at all? She is well-liked and her business did not hurt anyone. Yet, and most painfully, she sensed when she met some of her neighbors that they were pleased that her business had failed. Perhaps one might think that Celia's misfortune was simply the consequence of a conscientious government making sure that the laws are uniformly enforced. Much policing, however, comes from neighbors and "friends" who feel their poverty and oppression all the more when they see a fellow Cuban a little better off and a little freer, or maybe just with the prospect of being a little better off or a little freer. Probably very few take pride in being informants, but they also fear getting in trouble themselves for not having reported something they should have.

This attitude builds on another inconsistency. The government is corrupt. Corrupt not in the free-wheeling and pseudo-democratic style found in pre-revolutionary Cuba and much of Latin America, but with a tightly held venality. At the Marina Hemingway, named for the author the government has almost adopted as Cuba's own, where many foreigners and a very few Cubans keep their pleasure boats, luxury goods are easily available. Also much in evidence are the adolescent and twenty-something children of the communist elite. They can be seen, ironically, drinking Cuba Libres and complaining about shortages and lack of travel opportunities. Never far away, especially in the evenings, are prostitutes who have bribed their way in in the hope of finding a "date" for the evening.

As in all communist countries, there is a clear class system in Cuba. Given the experience of Communism in Eastern Europe, it is to be expected. What is surprising is the imitation of so much of the worst of the "colonial" situation before Castro, tourist apartheid, prostitution and repression being the most obvious. While Cuba has very limited direct trade with the U.S., and vice versa, it can trade with the rest of the world. Few, if any, products that Cuba produces lack some international market, and hardly an item Cubans would buy is not available from Canada, Europe, Latin America, Japan or some other country. There is no lack of trading partners.

Cuba is a poor country for two reasons. Being small and lacking a variety of valuable natural resources in high demand, until recently it has always had a principal partner. At first it was Spain, then the U.S., then the Soviet Union, and now it is no one. In this sense, as Wayne Smith, a former U.S. Chief of Mission in Havana and Director of the Johns Hopkins Cuba Exchange Program, has observed, Cuba has finally achieved its independence. Secondly, a command economy under one man rule has everywhere produced poverty — even in a country like Cuba, which was one of the wealthiest countries in the Caribbean before the Communist revolution of 1959. Today the only country in the Caribbean poorer than Cuba is Haiti. This is not to say that the pre-revolutionary wealth was equitably distributed, or that the U.S. embargo on trade with Cuba is a politically wise or humane policy, only that the embargo is not responsible for Cuba's misery.

Class distinctions and backbiting are not the only sources of self-directed anger in Cuba. The old divisions of family and region, for example, continue, now amplified. Hernando, a heavyset young man in his mid-forties, owned an art gallery, as did his father, who died in 1999. Hernando knew the country well as he traveled throughout the island, buying paintings, sculptures and old post cards. Hernando is one of the most cosmopolitan and informed Cubans I know, and as he hoped to be able to sell some of this material on the world market, he was very interested in American politics. The North American Free Trade Area is described in the Cuban government media as a link in the chain of neo-liberal slavery, but those Cubans looking the future show a more positive interest. Castro is of course a key part of any political equation there. I asked, "If things were different"—a code phrase in Cuba for "after Communism"—"would there be support for Cuba being in NAFTA?"

"It's hard to say." he replied. "What about support today for Castro?" I asked. "No one knows for sure how much political support for"—here he made the sign of the beard, "there is." He mentioned the "surprise" electoral ousting of the pro-communist government in Nicaragua in 1992. "It's one thing with the government press and all that now, but who knows if there was an open election."

I continued to press him. "But how much support do you think he has?"

"Maybe about thirty percent. Out in the country conditions are somewhat better than before the revolution, and they don't envy the Habaneros any more. You know, we Cubans like to complain but no one does anything."

He paused then, as if he were considering whether he should say more, and then did. "Once (beard gesture) is no longer around, then everyone will begin to make their moves." He went on to note that the rural folk are also more self-sufficient, and as a result can better withstand the bottom falling out of the economy. Add to that their isolation and the fact that they have much less of an idea of what is going on in the world, and they can consider themselves pretty fortunate. Perhaps ignorance is bliss after all.

By Cuban standards, the last few years had been very good for Hernando. His well-deserved reputation for honesty, his excellent English, and his good nature opened many doors for him. Among the many artists he knew, he was much respected. In 1997 he opened a gallery in Old Havana, where modern works were sold on consignment. As tourism expanded, so did his business, and his reputation and that of his gallery traveled far. He was selling plenty of paintings and sculptures to tourists and diplomatic personnel stationed in Havana. He got his own e-mail account, and, with the help of some Canadian friends, set up a website for the gallery. A year later he had bought a new house, a detached building of several rooms just outside of Miramar. His friends in many embassies helped him get visas, and he traveled often to Spain, Italy and the U.S., where he would sell paintings in galleries at even higher prices than back home. To many artists he was much like a savior. One day, working on the computer, he heard footsteps coming down the hallway. Getting up to greet yet another client, he instead was coldly met by two government officials. Showing him an official decree, they informed him that his gallery, and all the other "independent" galleries, were now closed. No ifs, ands or buts. If he did not close up immediately he would be fined severely. They then left without any further words. The pendulum had swung yet again.

Later, Hernando related to me how he felt dizzy, and sick. He closed the door behind the officials, sat down, and cried. With the stroke of a pen, his whole life had crumbled. What would he do now? How would he provide for his family? Sure, he had some good savings, but that would only last several months. Maybe this was just some warning, and the order would be reversed. He knew better, though: these things may change, but only years later. He could not think clearly, yet somehow he had always known deep down inside that this would happen. A few days passed, and he met with a good friend in the U.S. Interests Section. Three weeks later he was granted a visa to come to the U.S. for three months. He would be separated from his wife and two adolescent children, but at least he could still bring paintings out and sell them in the gallery of some friends in California. This, he knew, was only a stopgap measure, because given what had happened, a prohibition on the export of paintings might not be long in coming. In the meantime, he would just continue to try to survive, to save and to hope for a change. He could not bear the thought of leaving his wife and children, nor that of working in some government job.

I have also found that the people in Havana and in the western part of the island generally do not care too much for those, like Castro, from the east of the country. This is a recurring theme. The Habaneros complain that the people from the east are pushy and aggressive. Sitting in his small, cramped apartment one day and talking about this, Felipe said that he would not want any house guests from the east. "They would just move in and take over. They would say they have nowhere else to go, and they wouldn't leave. The next thing you know, I would be the one looking for a roof over my head. This happened to a friend of mine in Old Havana."

For most foreigners, there is Havana and then there is the rest of Cuba. But Cuba is as rich in regions as it is in people. And as in many countries, things are often more interesting once you get out of the capital. In 1998, when Hernando was still permitted to buy and sell art, he and I linked up with Felipe for a trip south across the Island, to Batabanó. Felipe, with his tourist connections, was to get the driver and automobile. I was eating breakfast under the stained glass and Moorish arches of the musty, shabby Inglaterra Hotel just at the edge of Old Havana when Felipe arrived to tell me that he had landed an Oldsmobile. Being an Olds owner myself, I was delighted, once again amazed at his abilities, and I started to relax under images of a nice sedan with air conditioning and plush seats. After a last swig of my coffee, black and sweet as a Haitian friend of mine likes his women, we headed outside. Going around the corner and discreetly entering the car, I hoped Felipe and our driver, Esteban, did not sense my disillusionment when I saw our conveyance, a pre–Castro, maybe even pre–Eisenhower, sedan, irregularly spray-painted outside, the floor of the front seat heavily patched with fiberglass.

Of course I should have known better: Cuba is the world center of mobile automotive antiques. Studebakers must have been terrific cars, or at least very popular in Cuba in the 1950s, for you see a great many of them. Ernest Hemingway left one of his gardeners (who also acted as chauffeur) his 1959 Chrysler. Collectors have offered over fifty thousand dollars for it, but the owner may only legally sell to the government (who would then perhaps re-sell it or put it into commerce as an upscale taxi), and he and now his heirs refuse to do so. Today, it is among the many ancient Chryslers being gently driven on the streets of Havana. (Hemingway left his fishing boat, the *Pilar*, to the man who took care of and captained it. This heir did sell it to the government, and it is on display at the Hemingway house.)

The four of us got in the ancient Olds and it pulled out from the curb, alternately wheezing, grinding and grumbling, with an exhaust plume that rivaled that of the oil refinery across Havana Bay. The question of air conditioning did not arise, not only because the car probably never had it, but also because only two of the windows were capable of going up. On reaching the open road we knew we had attained cruising speed when all four doors began to rattle violently and the steering wheel jerked from side to side. Unlike the "*Ocho Vias*" or eight lane highway which goes lengthwise across much of the island, this road did not have abandoned trucks in the left lane, nor detours by which you are sent against traffic and whose ends are not marked, leaving the unwary driving the wrong way down the highway.

It was a wonderful trip, over low undulating hills to the ocean. The roads were good, and there was hardly any traffic. There was a problem with the fuel supply, however, and every fifteen miles or so we had to stop. Esteban would hop out, pop the hood, take a two-gallon fuel container that was secured with a chain under the hood and connected to the carburetor, and refill it by siphoning fuel from the original tank in the rear. Then he would replace the can on its perch next to the radiator and pop in the hose to the carburetor, and we would lurch off again. During these interludes, we were often approached by groups of people selling garlic strands and cheese along the side of the road, desperate forays into a glutted market.

Cubans are warm and friendly people, with a keen and often subtle sense of humor. Among the many island peculiarities that I found appealing were the different ways Cubans address one another. Two that come to mind are "Animal" and "Monster." These terms are meant in somewhat of a flattering tone, as we might say "Hey, big guy." Still, such addresses must be used with caution, even with a smile. If you do not know the person, they can be misinterpreted as fighting words. The trick is to follow up quickly with a question or comment. Felipe demonstrated this extensively on the trip to and around Batabanó. Road signs are not clear in rural Cuba, so Felipe, Esteban, Hernando, and I found ourselves asking and confirming directions a lot. Felipe generally addressed people as "Animal," telling me that as one heads to the east there is a gradual shift to "*Monstro.*" I stuck to "Señor."

Batabanó is your typical small, desolate beachfront town, with wooden shacks and deserted streets. Perhaps that explains why the beach was so crowded. We spent some time there and then drove a bit around town. Soon Esteban was pulled over by a cop on a motorcycle, his hand resting on the gun slung low on his waist as he walked to the car. Felipe, Hernando, and I just sat tight, hoping he would not start to ask a lot of questions for which the truth might not be a possible answer. While some Havana police wink at black market rentals, we were quite a way from Havana. We looked at each other in consternation when the policeman, his lips as tight as his uniform, ordered Esteban to raise the hood, and began to criticize him sharply for his creative fuel tank. He then began to point at the cracked spark plug wires and frayed belts. I was not aware that proper vehicular maintenance was a measure of revolutionary zeal, nor that they had roving motor inspectors. As Cuban cars go, this one was not out of the ordinary. After defensive explanations and apologetic overtures from Esteban, the hood closed with a resounding clang, and he got back in the car, sweating not just from the heat. It turned out that Esteban had bought the car from the father of the policeman, and the cop remembered it, having ridden in it as a child. Esteban was set loose after promising to do the necessary repairs, with the threat that the cop would have his relatives check on him in Havana.

The way the policeman treated Esteban was typical of how many government officials treat others, even in professional relationships. Distrust is based on fear, and professional relationships are, with few exceptions, devoid of any warmth or trust. There was only one way that I saw to cut through all of this, and that was to get a patron, a protector. In November of 1998 I brought several congressional staff members to meet with a broad group of Cubans, including dissidents. During that trip, having been invited to make some comments to a commission of the National Assembly, I happened to meet one of the original comandantes of the revolution, Jesús Montané. At the conclusion of our brief meeting, he offered to meet with me the next time I was in Cuba. I followed up, and a couple of months later did meet him. Thanks to this encounter, I finally found a way to easily get past the functionaries who run immigration and customs at the airport. When they growled at me demanding the purpose of my visit, I simply told them I was here to meet Comandante Montané. "Well, come on in, sir" was the usual response.

Montané and I met in his office in the presidential palace, a nearly deserted complex that had the cool, quiet, spacious and empty feel of a huge mortuary. Despite looking tired, he was welcoming and courteous, something new to me after dealing with so many Cuban government officials. Montané had seen it all, including the Moncada attack. He was one of the real survivors who I can only hope saw the contradictions of the monster he had labored so hard to create. In his seventies, he remained active, though nearly deaf, visiting the provinces, taking on special projects and, like everyone else, trying to bring needed foreign exchange into the country. In Cuba, he had not only formal authority, but an unspoken moral authority. He was more open than many others, and for the next couple of hours I screamed in his ear, he screamed in mine, and his secretary/bodyguard wrote it all down, perhaps almost deaf himself from listening to so much shouting. We talked about his interest in African American spirituals, his struggles, victories and defeats, the challenges the country faced, and how difficult it was to operate programs such as mine. I told him to check me out, which I am sure he had already done or I would not have been there, and stressed that my work had benefits to both peoples. Whether you liked or agreed with him or not, he had led a very interesting life. As dusk fell, I took my leave, and we agreed to meet the next time I was in town. I felt I was on the way to having a court of appeal the next time I needed one. Unfortunately for me, and for him, I read a few weeks later that he had died, reportedly from an allergic reaction to shellfish. It was a good thing that I heard about it before I returned to Cuba. It would not have gone over very well in immigration if on the next trip I were to have told them that I was going to see El Comandante Montané.

Nearly all the leaders of the revolution are venerated. Perhaps people admire their courage, their intentions, their stated ideals. No doubt, people so frustrated by living in such a poor and unnecessarily marginalized country need heroes. During one of my stays in Cuba, the remains of Castro's fellow revolutionary, Ché Guevara, which had lain in an unidentified grave in Bolivia for about thirty years, were brought back to Cuba. The way the repatriation was handled was surreal. It was as if he were still living and now had returned, quite exhausted, after a long trip. One government official told me that Guevara was "resting" in the Ministry of Defense. Later, another told me that he would be "continuing his journey" to Santa Clara, where a mausoleum-*cum*-shrine had been built for him. But rather than a rest, it might have been more appropriate to say that he had been sent into internal exile. It was obvious that Castro did not want too much attention lavished on Guevara. To borrow a phrase, Guevara's death was a smart career move. He could only be associated with the hopeful early days of the revolution, not its messy and disappointing aftermath.

Serena, a middle-aged professor of Latin American art history at the University of Havana, would sometimes cock her head approvingly at one of Havana's many stylized murals of Guevara. But I noticed that she never said or indicated anything about Castro. I never asked direct or even leading questions about politics to academics in Cuba. Unlike academics I have known everywhere else, they are reluctant to express any opinions except the party line, although their silences or indirect comments can be illuminating. Once, Serena was a guest at one of the dinners in Havana's Old Town that my Institute had arranged for some academics from the United States. Afterwards, the other guests had gone their own way to walk around or to their hotels. Serena and I were walking over to a taxi stand near one of the tourist shops when she happened to see a Jesus-like picture of Guevara decorating a coffee mug.

Pulling a long face, she said, "Is this how he would want it?" I was noncommittally silent, letting her speak if she wanted to. "Castro's smart," she said after a longish pause, in what I thought was a curious change of subject. "You don't see pictures of him on walls or on coffee mugs. Of course there is no cult of personality with him." Here she raised her eyebrows and looked at the sky in a gesture that indicated that the statement was ironic. "You know how some people like to stand out by being plain when everyone else is flashy. And the flashy ones look...," and here she shrugged her shoulders. And then just so I got the point, "But only Fidel makes the big long speeches."

As she mentioned his capacity for speechmaking, an errant thought ran through my mind. Could it be that for speech topics he just thinks how messed up things are at home and substitutes "the United States" for the word "Cuba"? How else could he go on so long? Yet it would be wrong to think that Serena does not admire and respect Castro. Despite her down-to-earth no-nonsense personality, she often displayed an emotional attachment to Castro and to the other leaders of the revolution. Once, speaking of Camilo Cienfuegos, another revolutionary leader, she muttered, almost to herself, "They were heroes. All of them. Heroes."

Cubans hate their chains, but they respect, even love, those who forged them. Elderly people, like the very young, tend to be outspoken everywhere. This is the case in Cuba as well. Chiquita, as everyone calls her, is a ticket taker in a movie theater. She was twenty in 1959, when Castro came to power. It is natural that people idealize their youth, and in her case it does seem like a charming youth. You could still see that she had been very pretty — she also assured me several times that that was the case — and she had lived a pleasant life as the daughter of the owner of a photography shop in the lovely provincial city of Trinidad, on Cuba's south coast. She and her husband had divorced in the early 1970s — though she spoke well of him. She had not been a fighter in the revolution, but like almost all Cubans had enthusiastically supported it when it came. "It was the future, one that we were creating. It was hope in action. Young people love the future." But when the subject of Castro came up she would frown and begin to grumble loudly about how hard things are now. Once, when I was talking with her at her apartment, Castro began to make a speech on television. I waited, expecting the usual outburst. But she stared at the screen, enraptured. She clearly adored the man.

"La Barba" does have a grip on his subjects, many grips. He is charismatic, and what people in the U.S. often don't understand is that to the Cubans, and many Latin Americans, he is a patriot first and a communist second, a hero first and an oppressor second. For this reason they respect him, even if they resent him. The Cuban revolution is also idealized by many in other Latin American and African countries, mostly for standing up to the United States. This, along with basic health care and high levels of literacy, is a source of pride for many Cubans. The problem is that they have few means of comparing it with anything other than what the Cuban government tells them. This they accept with a skepticism they hope to abandon, and try it out on foreigners. If they can convince a foreigner it is true, then it must be. The trouble is that most foreigners arrive in Cuba seeing only what they want to see, eager to lay blame across the Florida Strait. In the end, Cuban skepticism prevails, but only slightly. They want to believe what their government tells them, they have to repeat it, but in the end many know that it is all a fraud, and that they live in the dark.

It sometimes seems that the revolution is the Cubans' religion, while the United States is their promised land. It is a great irony that on the whole the Cuban people love Americans, and I mean *love* them. When someone finds out that you are their neighbor to the north, they often light up, and are even more welcoming than usual. Forty-some-odd years of anti–American, nationalist rhetoric have not made a dent, just as they did not in Eastern Europe. Forty-some-odd years of our trying to squeeze and starve the government into submission have not alienated them. I have only met one or two Cubans who support the embargo. Most see the embargo as misguided, but they do not resent the United States for it.

Once, I was getting into a black market cab, a 1955 Chevrolet, having been persistently coaxed by a tag team of a driver and his assistant, probably brothers, given the similarity of their appearance. The older one sat in the back and I the driver in the front. The car shuddered and lurched, and where glue failed miracles held. Most old American cars there have experienced extensive surgery, amputations and transplants over the years; many now even have Russian-built Lada engines. Designed for the Soviet equivalent of a Fiat sedan, these are not as powerful as the originals, but they consume a lot less gas. As Cuban cars go, this one was a near virgin. The two loved their car, the driver proudly announcing that it was "all original" as he struggled to control the steering wheel, which had a mind of its own. Even the spark plugs seemed to be original. The two young men were curious about where I was from, and when I told them the U.S., the one in the back seat gave a huge sigh of relief, as if by simply sitting in the car I was going to make things better. He then asked when we, I guess meaning the U.S. military, were going to come in and put an end to this craziness, while making the international sign of the beard. I told him that we had already tried that, and that it was their problem and up to them. That was not what he was hoping to hear, but he understood perfectly and reluctantly agreed. Most Cubans know where their problem is.

In small ways as well as in large Cubans show their attachment to the United States. Once Felipe asked me to bring him a shirt with the American flag on it on my next trip. He assured me that it would be OK, and that many people were wearing them. On my next trip, just to be safe I turned the T-shirt inside out and put it in the bottom of my luggage. Fortunately my luggage was not hand searched at the airport. It seemed that the pendulum had swung rather far in this respect; the swing the other direction could not be long in coming.

The one place in Cuba where Americans seem not so well liked is among the immigration officials. Wearing their olive-drab guayaberas and checking passports, they give each departing passenger the death stare, trying to make them break down and confess, to what I don't know, without saying a word. I have found the women officials somewhat more pleasant to deal with: their death stare is more one of simply suspicion. Once, going through the metal detector, I was carrying several boxes of cigars, some old art for which I needed and had an export permit, and, given that I set off the alarm, who knows what else. The only thing the officials insisted on seeing was the receipts for my cigars, to prove I did not buy them on the black market. No matter that I had several items of national patrimony, and perhaps other dangerous items. They stared at the receipts and boxes of cigars as if they had never seen such a thing before, proud that they had detected them but uncertain what to do next. You can never really relax until you are past the lone guard at the steps of the plane waiting to pluck passengers off like rejects on an assembly line, and have arrived at your destination. The immigration officials may be unpleasant, but the departure gate dynamics at the airport are heart-wrenching. There you will see scores of families making tearful good byes, some ready to collapse, and others to explode, with anguish, hugging and having other sobbing relatives pry them away.

The overall Cuban affinity for Americans is repaid in kind, and is shown by the American public's interest in the island. It is an interest that has steadily grown into a fascination, and for some an obsession. The explosive popularity of Cuban music, and culture more generally, has re-ignited a latent interest in Cuba that has developed into a fever. If culture has been the fire, the cigar craze of the 1990s was the smoke, and a lot of people resent not being able to get their hands on some good habanos. As an aside, it's worth mentioning that Cuban cigars are of tremendously varying quality. Whether it is civil disobedience, lack of incentives, soil depletion or excessive production demands, a box of habanos will almost certainly have plenty of bad apples and maybe a few weevils and some fungus. If you buy them on the street, they probably will not be what they appear. A good cigar may have a Cohiba ring, but that does not a Cohiba make. Whatever it is, however it is most likely to be very strong.

Music, culture and a general cigar craze only accentuated the fact that people could look, but not touch. You can read about Cuba, you can listen to Cuban music, you can go to a Cuban movie, you can even pretend to smoke a cigar with a Cuban name, but with few exceptions, you can't go to Cuba legally. Many, perhaps over 30,000 a year, do go without authorization from the U.S. government. They risk a heavy fine and a long jail term in their quest to taste the forbidden fruit. Those who go and those who want to go are ever more questioning of why they aren't allowed to. They see us trading with Vietnam, granting most-favored nation trading status to China, they see that Cuba is not the threat it once was, and are left scratching their heads.

The embargo is enforced by the Office of Foreign Assets Control

(OFAC), a part of the U.S. Department of the Treasury. OFAC also administers sanctions against other nations such as Libya and Iraq. In order to go to Cuba legally, those who are not government officials, professional journalists or researchers are required to have a license from OFAC. If the purpose of one's visit is consistent with the law and policy at the time, OFAC may issue a "specific license" which allows one to spend money in Cuba. (In an attempt to sidestep issues of freedom of association, the law does not prevent someone subject to American law from going to Cuba, only from spending money there.) If one is "fully hosted" by the Cuban government or someone not subject to American law, and consequently will not spend any form of currency there, one can go there legally. This also avoids the issue that most forms of association usually involve money, whether for a coffee, dinner or a phone call. In enforcing the law, the presumption is that those who traveled to Cuba have spent money, and the burden is on them to demonstrate otherwise.

In this process, Treasury is not bound by precedent, and as a result has a fairly free hand in determining to whom licenses are granted. If they are granted, it is usually at the last minute and after considerable pressure. Often it appears that there is a tacit desire on the department's past to be pressured. That way, if they grant a license and get heat from the Right as a result, they can respond that someone on the Hill or in the State Department was turning the screws to get it issued. There have been successful efforts to streamline the process, and the office does not appear to be adequately staffed to handle the number of requests they receive; but it is an extremely difficult and unresponsive bureaucracy to deal with. Many have complained that it is almost impossible to actually speak with a person there, and that calls are rarely returned in a timely manner if at all.

OFAC has a difficult and unpopular task. In a poll conducted in May of 1999, it was revealed that 71 percent of Americans support the renewal of full diplomatic relations with Cuba, "the largest margin of support in the past quarter of a century."* As early as 1974, 63 percent of Americans supported such a change. Concerning trade with the island, in 1994 35 percent supported ending the embargo, and by 1999 those supporting trade became a majority, at 51 percent. In a national poll in 2001 this number remained largely unchanged at 52 percent, although 63 percent viewed trade as the best way to promote a transition on the island. In the same

---

*David W. Moore, "Americans Support Renewed Diplomatic Relations with Cuba Although Majority Still Feels Negatively Toward the Country." Gallup News Service, appearing in Cuba Information Access (Internet), May 24, 1999.

poll, 66 percent supported allowing Americans to travel to the island, 75 percent supported the sale of medicine to Cuba, and 71 percent favored the sale of food to Cuba.*

All of that, however, was before "Little Elián," the sacrificial lamb to be devoured by the lions of the Right and Left, arrived in Miami. The sordid tale had three outcomes. One was that the American people found a way to express their frustration with the present policy. They were united on the subject as never before: the kid should be with his father; and they had a clear target, the Right. And they won. The second, and related, outcome was that the saga really irritated many other immigrant groups, not just in Miami but throughout the U.S. If Elián had been from Haiti he would have been lucky to spend the night in a detention center. There are many immigrants who are separated from their parents, but they are not offered millions to immigrate, or given a hearing by the Supreme Court.

The third outcome was that the Right was so busy hammering away that they failed to recognize that it was their own coffin they were at work on. When Miami Mayor Carollo announced that he would not assist federal officers in removing Elián from the custody of his relatives, he outraged a lot of people, and images of the American flag flying upside down in Miami sent them over the edge. A lot of Americans asked themselves, "Who do these people think they are?" The longer it dragged on, the more fed up people became, here and in Cuba, and the more resentful they became. That is why, when the order finally came to let him go to Cuba, the leadership of the Cuban Right decided not to close the city and Miami airport with protests. They had done enough damage to themselves already.

Despite the changes in American public opinion, the fact that Cuba is a forbidden isle perhaps remains its greatest attraction. It is an island behind a veil, and like thinking about a woman in a chador, people often let their imaginations run wild, enhancing the beauty concealed beneath. But when the veil is lifted, it is often shock and disappointment that greet the beholder, not beauty and unbridled passion. Cuba is no different. Certainly, it is a beautiful place, with a rich and varied culture. The people are open, unreserved and friendly, and love America and Americans. It is also a sensuous abyss of temptation, boiling with stimulation. Any place that is warm and produces the finest rum, good cigars, and lots of beautiful women has to be on many men's short list for paradise. And many who spend a few days there see this veneer, but never penetrate the complexity of the place. Cuba is like the looking glass in Alice in Wonderland. You can spend your time looking at the reflection, which is what most

*Rasmussen Research, poll conducted April 10–12, 2001.

people do, or you can walk through to the other side. Once you do so, you can appreciate the depth of the society, both good and bad.

Crossing the divide reveals many riches. Most things in Cuba you have to ask for. For example, to make sure the government restaurants have something to serve, the paladars, or private restaurants, are not allowed to serve shellfish, beef and many other foods. Sitting down and reading the menu, you will be greeted by a host of pork and chicken dishes. But if you say, "Thanks for the menu, but what else do you have to eat?" you will be presented with another, oral, menu, which may include lobster, alligator, turtle, beef and who knows what else. The same is true in some art galleries. Once, I went into one gallery, and spent a few minutes looking at the usual tourist art. I asked the gentleman if he had any other works for sale. He did, and led me through his gallery, down an alleyway, through a house and to a room that was literally full to the rafters of landscapes, abstracts and other art, much of it from before the revolution. Had I not asked I never would have seen what lay on the other side.

While getting past reflections often reveals hidden beauties, it also reveals the sadness and misery that weighs on the Cubans. Cuba is a sad place, where people don't just lack opportunity, they are deprived of it. They have learned not to trust one another and few dare to express their hopes. They wonder where their next meal is coming from, and know that whatever it ends up being, it probably will not satisfy. With empty words, they parrot the lines that will keep them out of trouble. In many ways it is like other poor countries which dot the globe. What makes it worse, however, is that it does not need to be that way. Cuba is a rich country, especially in terms of its human resources, and when reason finally prevails there, it will rapidly achieve its potential. In the meantime it is like someone living in penury who has not been notified that he has a generous inheritance waiting. Those who do cross the divide will also find that Cuba is in effect a small town of eleven million. As anywhere, after a while, things start to repeat themselves, and the clichés get a bit worn. So many pictures of Castro walking in the jungle, of Ché Guevara staring defiantly, of salsa, rumba, spandex and mojitos.

In their naïveté and desire to feel like "one of the people," many visitors confuse their experience with that of those who live there. The people rarely say what they really feel about the regime, they speak in code, and sometimes they try to convince themselves by trying to convince others that they actually like it: the romantic visitor may never get a sense of what people are up against or how they feel. If you want to know what a Cuban thinks about a sensitive topic, ask him or her what other Cubans think, and you will get an earful.

Often these same visitors confuse the stated ideals of the revolution with its practice. That is one of the great ironies of communism. The system that supposedly cares most about human welfare is the one that has stripped people of their civil rights and dignity and failed to provide the basics. And the system that is wholly impersonal, subjecting everything to the merciless discipline of the market, is the one that has provided the most opportunity to the most people and the highest standard of living in history. Many visitors believe in the ideals of the revolution, and, like Columbus, confuse what they see with what they want to see. And, if they see something that they simply can't ignore, such as people selling themselves, or a building in Old Havana falling apart, then they attribute it to the embargo. It is an exercise in selective perception.

In the end, the American people have a lot to offer Cuba. Americans find the island alluring, and when the chador is finally removed and the mystique is unmasked, they will find there is still plenty to do and appreciate there. But whatever we have to offer the Cubans, we have to be able to offer it. In a diffuse way, the Right has done to other Americans what it has done in much of its own community, and what Castro has done in Cuba: imposed censorship, stifled discussion and limited information. The average American can't go there, can't gather information and can't base an opinion on firsthand experience. Nor can they share with the Cuban people some of the things we have to offer, such as a deep-seated and well-justified suspicion of government, a disrespect for unjust authority, and the example of a system that likes to see other people succeed.

CHAPTER 5

The Long Road to Pluralism

I have known and worked with many people, from many parts of society, in Cuba. Much of my work there was with university administrators, faculty, government officials, and leaders of non-government organizations. Next to that group, I had extensive dealings with the United States government (especially the Department of the Treasury and the Department of State) and Tulane University. Everything to do with Cuba is complicated. This book is not about the United States, but about Cubans. The reader can be assured, however, that a good deal of what I describe about Cuban academic politics could also be applied to the United States. Let me say, however, that the United States Department of State, and especially its mission in Havana, was always an effective, honest, and forthright promoter of academic and cultural exchanges between the U.S. and Cuba. At Tulane, the administration, faculty and students were always enthusiastic supporters of the Cuban Studies Institute.

Tulane's Cuban program grew rapidly from a small study-abroad program to a series of academic and cultural exchanges of faculty, administrators, students, performers and citizens from New Orleans and elsewhere. In 1995 I decided to follow up on some contacts I had earlier made at the University of Havana to see if they would be interested in hosting a summer session as a step toward creating a full-time semester or year program in Cuba with American students going to classes and rooming with Cuban students. I recognized that there would be problems establishing and maintaining such a program — though Tulane, like many other universities, has such programs in a wide variety of countries. Still, the best way for students to learn about a country and develop facility in that country's language is to spend an extended period of time there. A summer program would be a good start, a trial run — in more ways than one, as I came to discover — for the more ambitious program.

Just as our government let these students go to Cuba in the hope of promoting the flow of ideas into the country, the Cuban government received them, and their money, in the hope that they would return to the U.S. and agitate for an end to the embargo. Some students who were perhaps sympathetic upon arrival soon saw the situation for what it is: the product of an irrational economic system, made worse by the Soviet cutoff and, to a limited extent, the embargo. Perhaps the best way to cure someone of communism is to send them to a Communist country. African-American students quickly had their illusions of a racial paradise dashed when they were refused entry into their own hotel until they could demonstrate they were Americans. One year, some students saw the police state in action when two teenagers they were palling around with were stopped by plainclothes police, separated, questioned, and taken away in an unmarked car. In the end, while very few students were fond of Castro's management style, after some time on the island most did think the embargo either punished the innocent, was ineffective, or just gave Castro someone else to blame for his economic woes. I would not chalk such sentiments up as a victory for his propaganda machine, because a great number of people in the U.S. who have never been to Cuba also share these views.

Cuba is a contact sport, and the embargo is one of the balls that gets kicked around, along with the players. On the one hand, like a tarp over a rainy crime scene, the embargo clearly benefits Castro as a means of covering up the wreckage of his economy. If it were to be lifted, however, he would also benefit, not only because "he won," but also because the economy would improve somewhat and a lot of the economic pressures would be taken off him. It is a lot easier to run a police state when the economy is working. It may well be, as many have argued, that Castro really doesn't want the embargo lifted. He's been running things with it for over forty years, while being able to point a finger of blame at the U.S. We should not ignore the role of pride here in perpetuating the situation. There is a saying in Spanish which translates as "Two big noses can never kiss," and when it comes to relations between Cuba and the United States, both governments have big noses indeed.

There are other considerations concerning the embargo. During a conversation on American policy towards Cuba, I once asked a Mexican friend if he thought that Mexico should be obligated to trade with the United States. Indignant, he exclaimed that Mexico was a sovereign nation, that they are the ones who determine who their trading partners are, and that no one has the right to force them to trade or not trade with anyone. It is no different with the United States and Cuba. It may be a misguided policy, but it is our decision. The United States is not a big department store where every nation of the world has the right to shop and sell their wares. If we choose not to maintain trade relations with a particular country, and shoot ourselves in the foot in the process, to paraphrase Fats Waller, "Ain't nobody's business if we do."

Still, it is fairly well demonstrated that embargoes are not effective in removing governments; and while they are not working, they squeeze the poor and middle classes and give the government a clear enemy to blame. In Panama, it took a full-scale military invasion to get rid of Manuel Noriega, and Saddam Hussein has weathered the sanctions against Iraq for over a decade. The other thing is that there are well over 180 other countries in the world with which Cuba can trade. Not all have the same selection of stock on the shelves, but there is no shortage of shops in the mall. Where the embargo, largely defined, does put the screws on Castro is through blocking his access to international sources of money, such as the World Bank and other multilateral lending institutions. The Helms-Burton legislation, which provides for sanctions for companies that utilize expropriated assets in Cuba, has also been a misguided approach to securing international compliance with our policy. Not only has it peeved our major trading partners, but more importantly, through codifying a series of other laws, it severely limits the ability of the American president to exercise what historically has been his prerogative, the conduct of foreign policy. It has also added yet another arrow to Castro's quiver, allowing him to continue playing the role he plays best, the persecuted but defiant rebel.

There are, in the end, two simple reasons for lifting the embargo: it hasn't worked and it does not advance our national interests. Trade is the oyster shucker of closed societies, because it promotes the flow of people, information and ideas. The United States government encourages academic and cultural exchanges with Cuba to create such a flow. Trade is another, larger-scale means of doing the same thing. More importantly, it creates jobs on both sides of the divide. Trading with our adversaries is one of the best ways to defeat them. This was the case with the Soviet Union, and is the case with China and Vietnam.

Like many people who deal with Cuban government officials, I initially thought that I would be able to overcome their suspicions of me by focusing on common ground and executing projects successfully. I understood their misgivings: Their relations with the U.S. have been nothing but conflict, and the U.S. policy that promoted academic and cultural exchanges was explicitly predicated on overthrowing their government. I couldn't blame them for a bit of skepticism. Things are made worse, however, by their tendency to see everything in black and white.

Early on, Luís, a University of Havana administrator who was the gatekeeper for such programs, had been cautiously receptive. Increasingly, however, he had become reticent and did not respond to my calls or e-mail. Working in Cuba is not for the faint of heart or for the unassertive, so one morning I called to tell Luís that I was in Havana and would like to meet with him. He agreed to receive me, and at 11:30 I dropped in at the Office of International Relations, where he worked. I knew that a substantial part of the responsibility of that office was to prevent, not promote, international contacts with the United States. Coming from New Orleans, where office seekers commonly run on platforms promising not to do their job (tax assessors, and many legislators), I understood his situation, but I also knew that sometimes exceptions could be made. Luís was polite but seemed nervous and did not even offer me the customary cup of black coffee.

"Nick, I would like to talk with you, but it is best if you speak with my boss, Doctor Gómez. He wants to meet you."

I feared this was a bad sign, and probably the cause of Luís's recent distance. Dr Gómez, the Director of the Office, greeted me very cordially, offered me coffee, and told me that he had once visited Seattle, Washington, though he did not say why. But no sooner had I said how glad I was to meet him than he began to relate a detailed history of the university since its founding in 1728. Forty minutes into a daze conjured by his lecture, he had brought me all the way to the year 1810. He began to look disembodied, in a vacuum, his head wagging as his eyebrows danced above his brown eyes, greatly magnified by his glasses. Every time I tried to get a word in or ask a question, he would cut me off, taking refuge in even more detail.

I had plenty of time to appreciate his office, the starkness of which reminded me of a police station. But instead of bulletin boards and pictures of the most wanted, he had two framed pictures of Castro (certainly on the most wanted list in Miami), one at the time of the revolution and one somewhat more recent. On the opposite wall was a framed picture of Ché Guevara, whose body was then still unrepatriated. Other than these two pictures the walls displayed only announcements, written on poster board in bold, red letters, that the purpose of his office is to promote knowledge of the revolution, export the revolution, to continue to fight for the revolution, and to be ever vigilant of efforts to subvert the revolution.

Around the year 1860, I decided to jump in and ask about his vision of the future of the university. My effort was in vain. An hour later, in which I had said, or tried to say, no more than ten words, he announced that he was going to call the rector, or president, of the university, to see if he would receive me. The call was made in private, but I could see his relief when he returned and announced with pride that the rector would see me immediately. He could wash his hands of me, I was now his boss's problem.

We strolled over to the rector's office, which was in a grand, ochre, colonnaded building on a hill within view of the sea. It was January, and the chilly, damp wind tore through its central patio as we entered his suite. The rector, and about six of his assistants, were all dressed in heavy jackets, not only to protect them from the wind outside, but also from the needless air conditioning inside. We sat down, and I explained that I was there in the hope of building relations and collaborating with their great university, steeped in such a deep and rich history; that we had no political aims but would like to send American students there the following summer. I went on to describe Tulane, and presented him with a nice coffee table book on it, as a gift from my president. The whole while, he had a slight grin on his face, both bemused and skeptical. I felt he was thinking that he had just about figured me out: either I was crazy or worked for the Central Intelligence Agency. I was tempted to assure him that, yes, I was crazy, and, no, I did not work for the CIA, but felt that he might take that as proof positive that in fact I did work for the Agency, which I did not. Finally, he told me that we had to move "little by little, step by step" and that they were not ready to work with us. At first I was discouraged, but on thinking about it, decided it was a good beginning. I did get to see all the people who mattered, they were polite, and the president was positive, though not as positive as I had hoped.

If universities generally move slowly, the University of Havana very often does not move at all. As with almost all Cuban government officials, university administrators will rarely tell you no, and almost never tell you yes. Instead, they will lead you along with ambiguous statements or the delaying assertion that "We have to analyze this." No one will make a decision without consulting their boss, and he must consult his boss and so on. The result is near-paralysis, its code word "analysis." And then, when a decision is made, you will not be told until the last minute. And even then it will still be tentative as some unforeseen international event may make them change their minds. Add to the mix ignored calls, unanswered email and aborted faxes, and you get an idea of what it is like. So, you live with ambiguity and get used to managing crises. The fact that for some reason the university administrators don't communicate well with their other government agencies to get things done doesn't help either. People often think that communist systems are uniform and monolithic, but they aren't. Instead, like any political entity, they are fragmented with factional disputes and rife with resentments and turf wars. Castro encourages this, as it is a way to continually remind people that they must in the end come to him to have things resolved.

There was a distinct similarity between making arrangements at the University of Havana and getting a license for Tulane's Cuban activities from the United States Treasury Department. You had to maintain the urging in the face of near total silence, but somehow things always came together at the last minute. We would send draft syllabi to the university months ahead of time, requesting feedback and the names of professors. They would get back to us a week or two before arrival. One year they sent the final written grades three months after the class had ended. Poorly responsive units appeared to limit their cooperation to other poorly responsive units. Once, the University of Havana administrators strongly indicated that we should use a travel agency based at their university. We tried to accommodate them, but the university travel agency was not willing or able to offer any prices for travel, lodging, etc., in a timely manner. I quickly lost count of how many calls, emails, faxes and other messages we sent, receiving nothing but silence. Once, they gave us our reservations two days before a group was set to arrive. In the end, we just stopped using them.

In a dictatorial, monistic, bureaucratic state, an error by an official goes on his permanent record, and is more likely sooner than later to damage his career. It may even cost him his job in an economy where nearly all employment is by the government. The consequence is that individuals are rationally reluctant and even prudently unwilling to make any decision. If they do, and it turns out badly, they will not admit responsibility. It would be madness for them to do so, no matter how obvious the error. They cannot take responsibility for their actions, or, as is more often the case, their inactions.

The policy of the U.S. government did not made the problem of my Cuban counterparts easier. U.S. policy stateed that a goal of academic exchange is to subvert the Cuban government. Clearly, any Cuban working with Americans involved in academic matters must step very carefully. Moreover, the Cuban academics inevitably project their condition of employment onto their U.S. counterparts. They do not understand that, unlike in Cuba, universities in the U.S. largely do as they please, and their faculty often are outspoken in criticism of their own government. In my own case, the U.S. government gave contradictory signals. The U.S. Interests section in Havana was always helpful, as were the Congressional staffs. The U.S. Treasury varied between being intransigent and being unresponsive, as were many of the public statements of leading U.S. political figures. I knew that the sentiment within the New Orleans political establishment was also divided. So, each of us had our problems, which made it difficult to cooperate.

In a usually fruitless effort to have things go smoothly, I would go down to the island a couple of months early to meet with people, go over syllabi, finalize class schedules, etc. During one meeting, my counterpart asked if it would be all right to substitute a couple of sessions to develop the cultural nature of a class. That seemed to be a good idea, and I agreed. But upon arrival, with a dozen students in the class, they had not only changed those lectures as described, but had changed the title of the class and all of the other lectures as well. I was not the only one who was irritated; the students were as well. We all had been victims of a bait and switch. Students at Tulane and other universities earn credit toward their degree by taking specific classes to fulfill major and other requirements for graduation. Changes in the nature of the classes can significant major problems for them.

I insisted that we revert to the original agreement or cancel the class, and they honored the original agreement only after much resistance. A year later Luís was still complaining about it. Another class which we had organized for our students, on the business environment in Cuba, had been scheduled for the morning, but, without consultation, they decided to offer it in the afternoon. Many students had class conflicts as a result of this, so I also insisted that we offer it as planned. They did this only with the greatest reluctance. Professors often failed to show up for class, and it was not unusual for them to stand up students for scheduled excursions. It was irritating, but it was one of the many experiences that the students had that gave them a less romantic view of life under the revolution.

Part of any successful social interchange is the frequent acknowledgment of gratitude. Even when a waiter brings a dish to the table, patrons typically indicate thanks. Cubans outside government are warm, friendly, polite, and express a gracious thanks in appropriate circumstances just as people do all over the world. One of the things I noticed and was long puzzled by was their frequent unwillingness to do so in inter-university and government-related matters.

I would say to my counterpart at the end of a class term or the completion of a delegation's visit how much I appreciated his or her contribution and thank them for their help. They accepted the thanks, but did not acknowledge my or anyone else's contribution. For the most part, Cubans visiting New Orleans were more gracious, but even here the situation could be difficult. To facilitate future exchanges and to thank the university for its cooperation, we invited, at our expense, a high-ranking administrator to our campus. Older than many administrators, she had earned her stripes in the revolution as a young student activist. She described how, in the 1950s, students at the University of Havana were fed up with professors that they called "parrots" because they sounded like broken records. She also liked to relate how, over the bodies of their fallen comrades and armed with nothing more than sticks spiked with nails, they routed the old guard. I found it remarkable that she did not realize that what she was describing was not only the past, but also the present, and probably the future, and that she herself had become a "parrot." Like so many on both sides of the political equation, she was blind to the fact that she practiced what she condemned.

No sooner had she arrived in New Orleans than she started to criticize our marketing material, angry that we had sent it out without her express approval. She went on to criticize my assistant, and I later learned that she had earlier criticized me to my assistant. She insisted that her university take 50 percent of the profits of our program, though we already paid top dollar for all Cuban assistance and services. Somebody back home had probably briefed her to drive home the fifty/fifty policy on her grand tour, not that she really had any concept of what risks and costs went into organizing our part.

In a restaurant it was as if she had never had such a selection before her, and had little idea what any of it was. Her behavior reminded me of a child in a restaurant, a bit fidgety but trying to act grown-up. When the food arrived, she seemed to try to restrain herself from eating too fast. Later, arriving at a reception and dinner held in her honor, she entered the room and immediately asked in a loud voice, "Where are the cocktails?" She quickly drank two and became ever more loud, abusive, denigratory and morally righteous as the evening went on. Past midnight, she insisted that someone go out and buy a bottle of whiskey. The beauty of the embargo, and a reason for getting rid of it, is that you can blame anything on it. Our distinguished and soon to be unconscious guest had figured this out and even suggested that it was due to the "blockade" that she could not find a door hinge in Havana.

All universities from time to time have "visitors from hell." All countries produce such people. The style here is notable, however. She treated those with lower job descriptions at Tulane and the Cuban Studies Institute as she did those likewise placed at her own university. She seemed to think that she was a high-ranking administrator not only at the University of Havana, but at Tulane as well.

The uncertainty of working in Cuba was illustrated by the experience I had in connection with the delegation of congressional staffers I accompanied to Cuba in November, 1998. The problem began not with the Cubans, but with the United States Department of the Treasury. As government employees, the staffers did not need a Treasury license, but I did and so did two other Tulanians whose job was government liaison. Only after Treasury's congressional liaison office received a barrage of calls from the staffers' offices did we receive a license. It was granted about a week before departure, a record for promptness. One time, Treasury licensed a Tulane group three days after we were to have left. That way, if the trip were canceled, they could still say that they issued the license. The policy of Treasury, like that of the Cuban government, appeared to be to facilitate educational exchange reluctantly and minimally, and often to obstruct it, depending on the political winds of the day.

Organizing the congressional delegation, I met with the Cuban Interests Section in Washington, which functions as its embassy, and went over the itinerary in detail. They appeared eager to help make the trip a success, all the more so given the Republican contingent in the group. Although the delegation was largely composed of U.S. government employees, officers at the Cuban mission did not want them to visit anyone at the United States Interests Section in Havana. This restriction, I suggested, was unreasonable, as they were government employees and were not being sponsored by the Cubans. In the end, we compromised on an itinerary and had a list of participants which we all agreed upon. The day before departure, when I was literally packing my bag, I received a call from the Cuban Interests Section. They had a problem with the group. They only wanted the congressional staffers and me to go, not the other two Tulane participants. They claimed that they were under the impression that it was all staffers, and I had misled them. It was the usual maneuver: they had had the papers and résumés for over a month and we had even specifically discussed the two Tulane government liaison persons. I told them it was all or nothing, and we were getting on the plane and would go unofficially as tourists if that was what they preferred. They dropped the issue.

From New Orleans, a direct flight to Cuba would take about ninety minutes. Routing through Cancún can bring that hour and a half up to twelve hours. This time, avoiding Cubana's tottering Tupelovs, we took our chances on a vintage DC-10. Cancún airport is not my first choice of a place for a long layover. The air conditioning does work, some places, at some times, and the entertainment consists of either watching excited, scantily clad tourists get off the planes or watching pink, hungover, half-asleep tourists stagger back onto them with armloads of bulky hats and zarapes. Around this time there was a bit more intrigue than met the eye, however. As it turned out, the private company which ran security for the airport was working with drug traffickers. With their numerous hidden video cameras, they helped traffickers keep one step ahead in their eternal cat and mouse game with the Federal Judicial Police. It was later revealed that there was also a racket selling airplane fuel to the traffickers, who would truck it out to their airfields. The person who brought this to light was in the end murdered, and a high-ranking airport official was implicated in the killing.

On arrival in Havana, our reception at the José Martí International Airport was different than usual. Meeting us at the plane were both Cuban officials and the political officer from the U.S. Mission. We were immediately informed that the U.S. had resumed bombing Iraq because of Baghdad's refusal to allow continued inspections of their weapons facilities. Such actions by the United States worry the Cubans. It was, however, encouraging that the Cuban government sent representatives to meet us. They directed us to the VIP lounge while they collected, and presumably searched our luggage. On the other hand, our "handlers" were young and unkempt, speaking English well below the level of tour guides, not to mention official visitors. As we waited for the luggage, the taller of the two presented me with an envelope. Inside was a new itinerary. In this one, the delegation barely had time to go to the bathroom, much less walk around on their own, or, of course, visit with any American officials there. This was the usual routine.

I told them that we had two options: either we could all turn around and get back on the plane, or we could stick to the original agreement. They went on about how upset their bosses in the Foreign Ministry would be, how we really must accept the new itinerary, and how they are not responsible for the errors of their countrymen in D.C. I told them to tell their bosses that they had gotten this visit off to a very bad start, that I was disappointed that they would break their word, and that we were sticking to the original plan, whether they liked it or not. We collected our luggage and were off to our hotel. Over the next few days, we met with the usual people, in the Foreign Ministry, the Ministry of Agriculture, the Ministry of Investment, the Ministry of Commerce, etc. Some of the Foreign Ministry officials were apparently prone to Freudian slips, such as the one who greeted us with "welcome to our misery," instead of "ministry." Later, another noted the delays we often have with our Treasury licenses as a result of the officials at "the Department of Treachery." We also visited a children's hospital where we listened to a series of harangues asserting that the nation's medical problems are a result of the embargo, despite the fact that they can buy medicine from the rest of the world.

At breakfast in the hotel one morning, I inquired if two of the members of the delegation had had a pleasant jog. They said yes, they had. They added that they felt very safe here in Havana, especially as they noticed that they had been followed. At first they thought the moped a fellow was riding was just very slow, not unlike many street and sea spray-worn vehicles plying the streets of Havana. He had been behind them for several blocks, and then managed to gain enough speed to pass the joggers. About two blocks later his moped apparently broke down, and as they jogged by, he was hard at work making repairs. But just as they went by, he managed somehow to get it started, though was unable to go any faster then their stride. By the end of the jog, after he had again passed them up and again broken down, they were on friendly enough terms to wave to each other. One member of the delegation set up his luggage in such a manner that it would be clear only to him if someone looked through it. Sure enough, after a day of meetings, he came back to find that it indeed had been searched.

The U.S. Interests Section had set up a lunch with international journalists and businessmen, followed by a meeting with about a dozen of the leading dissidents. On the way to the home of the affable and indefatigable Chief of Mission, Michael Kozak, our Ambassador in all but name, our driver got lost. In fact, he got so lost that we arrived late to the luncheon. The residence is very grand, having been originally constructed to double as the American presidential winter White House in the 1930s. Set among five acres of lush grounds, it makes an imposing impression. Following lunch with the businessmen, the dissidents began to straggle in. They seemed resigned and worn down, yet somehow hopeful as for three hours and a half they shared their stories, their views, and their visions of the future. These were the people who would lead Cuba in the future, a diverse group of men and women of various ages. They existed at the sufferance of the government, as a demonstration of its "liberality." But they were nonetheless persecuted. Aside from their resistance to the regime, they also shared an appreciation for rum. Over the next few hours the gathering emptied several bottles. Not only did it help them relax, but no doubt also steeled them for their return to the real world patiently awaiting them on the other side of the gate.

What a sad life these people lead, refusing to be cowed and standing up for what they believe. Expressing thoughts that in the States might be material for a tepid op-ed piece requires the courage to accept the possibility of going to jail for several years. And even if they don't pick you up right away, they can at any moment, anywhere. These people spend their time in anticipation and dread, wondering when they will be hauled off or beaten by some "spontaneous" mob outside their decrepit apartment. The pressure on their families is great; anyone associated with them is not treated as well as a conformist. Perhaps to them the whole island is a jail, and prison is just one of its less pleasant cells. But clearly the comfort, the air conditioning, the rum, and the interest others had in their views sustained them that afternoon. What they wanted was plain: a democratic system with an economy that worked. That did not necessarily mean a society free of social conscience, but one that had room for the play of ideas. Every one of them believed that the embargo only gave Castro someone to blame.

I asked what they thought of academic and cultural exchanges. They were again unanimous in their support. The flow of ideas and people were like termites in Castro's house, and would inevitably aid in its collapse. I mentioned how elements of the Cuban American Right had spoken on their behalf, claiming that the dissidents supported the embargo and condemned exchange programs. They were surprised and not pleased. I told them not to worry; the extremist exiles pretend to speak for everyone else as well. Indignant, one independent journalist told me he was going to send out an article via the Internet stressing the importance of such exchanges. As the afternoon drew to a close, the last round of rum was accompanied by a lot of backslapping and picture taking. Soon they would be leaving the warmth of the cool mansion for the cold heat outside.

Later we attended a reception offered by the President of the National Assembly. It was a subdued affair, with some of the people we had previously met joined by a few other officials and crew-cut student "leaders." It was almost like a play, with the same actors playing the same roles, their lines only slightly muffled by the diaphanous veil of their masks. One of them was playing "Mr. President," looking reserved and formal, treated respectfully by his acolytes. President chosen by whom, I could only wonder from the audience. Why is it that everyone here seems to want to speak for everyone else? Why can't they just speak for themselves and respect the fact that not everyone will share their views? Another actor played the loose, affable expert on U.S. relations, and the student leaders, as stiff as the bristles on their heads, maintained a stern look of suspicion, a stance that had brought them where they were. It was an evening with the thought police, sweet and sour.

On our last night, we were scheduled to attend a play. Rumor had it that afterwards we were going to meet with Castro. On the way, we decided to stop at a place on the Malecón for a quick bite. As we sat at the plastic table, munching on our spongy pizza under the fluorescent lights, all of a sudden someone grabbed the purse of one of our delegates. It seemed in slow motion, and as I jumped up to try to intercept him, I was shoved from behind by another delegate, also trying to catch him. The thief was quick, sprinting half a block to where, as in a modern western, he jumped on the back of a waiting motorcycle and sped off against traffic. They were skilled in what they did: Apart from the fact that they were the proud owners of an American passport, a palm pilot, and a few hundred dollars, they also had, whether they knew it or not, a roll of film containing photographs, taken earlier that afternoon, of dissidents being friendly with Americans. The rest of the evening was spent consoling the victim, reporting the incident to the police, and getting some exit papers to replace the passport. In the end, we had to stand Castro up. The group had been great to travel with. They were young, insightful, asked tough questions, had great senses of humor and knew how to make the most of a situation.

I have often wondered if it was government agents who took the purse. It is certainly possible, given that we were tailed, and had just met with the dissidents, and could have been exporting some papers for them. Here we are under surveillance in a police state, a country that has low levels of crime against tourists, and we get robbed. In the end, though, I think it was simple theft. We stopped there entirely on the spur of the moment and the thief was already there and looked like he had been on the street for a while. The purse was irresistible. Upon arrival back in Cancún, another of the delegates noticed that not only was he missing a box of cigars, but had also "lost" a nice sport jacket.

It is difficult to tell just how much one is being observed by the Cuban security services. It is inevitable, given the history of U.S.-Cuban relations over the past forty-plus years, that all Americans, and especially someone like me, involved in academic exchanges, would fall under suspicion. I have never had anything to do with the Central Intelligence Agency — they have never even approached me. Surveillance is irritating, however, and offers and provocations from the Cuban side are common. This was especially so after a spate of bombings in hotels in 1998. At the Hotel Ambos Mundos one evening, just as I got into an elevator to go to my room, I was joined by a very chatty English-speaking clean-cut Cuban who said he was a researcher. I knew that if you're Cuban and do not work in the hotel, and you are in the hotel, then you most likely work for the internal security forces or are a prostitute, or both.

This fellow was a giveaway, as he had an accent that people only achieve after several years of training in language schools for government officials. Tune in to the English language program on Radio Havana and you will see what I mean; it strains to sound American, and has an exaggerated quality. Unwisely perhaps, and giving in to my curiosity, I agreed to have a drink with him at the beautiful rooftop bar. No sooner had we sat down than he confided in me that he has a lot of respect for the IRA and believed that setting off bombs is a great way to express one's political ideas. I simply responded that "I respect every nation's right to self determination and oppose violence in all its forms." The rest of the conversation was mined with similar traps, to all of which I responded similarly.

Over the next couple of weeks they tried other ruses, such as sending girls to my room and having strangers on the street and hotel employees ask me to take letters to the states to mail for them. A few days later, I ran into a former U.S. government official who had the room directly below mine in the hotel, and I know that a CNN reporter lived in the suite directly above my room. All of the rooms were alongside an unused elevator shaft. I guess that the rooms were wired in a cluster and reserved for "special guests."

The morning before I was to leave, they decided to give it one more shot. I received a call from a lady shouting into the phone, telling me that a "good friend" of mine had a car accident the previous night, and was unconscious in the hospital. She told me not to worry, though, because they would deliver "the papers" to me that evening, and asked where did I want to meet. I hung up, left the hotel and from another phone called my friend Felipe, who now also had a job at a night club. He was unconscious all right; he had gotten in from work at four a.m. and did not appreciate being awakened four hours later. In the end, it seemed that I had passed their battery of tests.

For the most part, however, the trip with the congressional staff delegation went fairly smoothly. But it's not as if it paid any dividends in Cuban political currency. Unlike any other Latin American country, there is no such thing as political capital there. You could lift the embargo, and they might say thanks, but the next morning they would not return your calls. There is no incremental building of trust, no pausing to appreciate joint accomplishments, no hints to subtly share information with you. You are always back at square one. Much of it results from the fact that these officials view the world conspiratorially, and like residents trapped in a haunted house in a B-movie, they are possessed by a siege mentality. I recognize that they are under attack, but in the end the way to escape is through negotiation, by making allies.

But their siege is not only from without, it is from within. Even the agents and enforcers of a police state need someone watching over them, tapping their lines, analyzing their comments and demeanor, watching for the subtlest of signs that they have been infected with a bourgeois mentality. And a bit of blackmail makes a fine chaser. There is always the Sword of Fidel hanging by a thread over their heads, waiting to come crashing down, reassigning their apartment, or car, or giving them some humiliating new job that tells them and all that know them that they have failed, that they are not pure. If they were to defect while abroad, any family left in Cuba would pay a heavy price for them.

The result is that they err on the side of caution, and over-interpret orders. If the word goes out to limit new academic programs, then they start to dismantle what is already there. The other effect is that they never want to expose themselves to the accusation that they are close to a foreigner. That would open the floodgates of imputation and wash away their whole delicate ecosystem of privilege. They are also constantly looking for signs of ideological or other weakness among their co-workers, an effort made easier by their tendency to socialize almost exclusively with each other. Naturally, being a tattle-tale is an effective way to prove your ideological purity. The result is like hungry piranhas in a shrinking pool, they eat each other.

Related to this are their attempts to outdo one another in their demonstrations of ideological firmness. It not only gives them a shield against attack, but also can help promote them. It is like listening to a group of people trying to out-curse one another. The whole charade perpetuates itself, although of course they must be careful not to overdo it, as that can raise doubts about how fervent they really are. All of this, on the personal, professional and societal level, destroys social trust. Indeed, these are the very strings which Castro so adroitly manipulates. Without them there would be much less fear, people would talk more openly, and the game would pretty much be over. Outside of government, even childhood friends never know when one will report what the other has said, out of revenge, in defense or in an effort to advance oneself. It is an efficient and effective system of control.

Showing how loyal they are to the revolution may help them avoid being stripped of rather modest privileges, or even advance their careers, but probably not to the point where they have any real decision-making authority. One reason Cuban government officials are so rigid is that they have no room for flexibility or any decision-making. Certainly, there are rules, which they will apply because if they don't they will get punished. But because they don't have any discretion in their application, rigidity becomes a form of self-validation. And the more rigid they are the more pure they are, defending the revolution against yet one more subversive assault. They never make a request, they just tell you what to do. By leaving no room for discussion and being unyielding they can not only save their hides, but also feel self-important.

This often enters the realm of the absurd. Once, exploring the possibility of organizing a sailing regatta between New Orleans and Havana (a project I disassociated myself from when it became clear we would not get a Treasury license), I discussed with one Cuban diplomat the arrival procedures, should any boats actually make it to Havana. This diplomat, who both looked and acted a bit like a belligerent bulldog, explained that when any boat was sixteen miles out from Cuba they should radio in to Marina Hemingway and announce their arrival. Simple enough. But, concerned that some right wingers from Miami might try to infiltrate the regatta, he assured me, while dramatically shouldering a bazooka in mime, that anyone who did not radio in would be promptly blown to bits. Fireworks from the Cuban welcoming committee.

Such authoritative attitudes do not differentiate Cuban bureaucrats from of their counterparts in many other developing countries, but in the latter there is usually room for a solution even if it takes a while to find. What makes Cuba different is the structure of the bureaucracy, because at whatever level you are, someone above you will be the one who makes the decision. Unless, of course, you are Castro. It is this that emasculates people. It is also why they will never tell you "no," and they will never tell you "yes," and why the government spends so much time "analyzing" things and in a state of paralysis.

Just as paralysis was common dealing with Cuban officials, so it was often when trying to get a license from Treasury. The congressional delegation did open a lot of doors back home, however. Most immediately, by being able to demonstrate that the Louisiana congressional delegation was supportive, it helped to expedite the license for another delegation I had arranged to take from New Orleans to promote cultural relations with Cuba. New Orleans shares more history with Cuba than perhaps any American city. One of the founders of the city, Pierre LeMoyne, Sieur d'Iberville, died and was buried in Havana. In 1764, the city came under Spanish dominion and began to report to Havana. Cubans always like the thought that a part of what is today the United States was subordinate to them. It was not a match made in heaven, however. In 1769, the new Spanish governor dispatched from Havana, Alejandro O'Reilly, was in New Orleans for only four months before the locals ran him out. In an early charter of the University of Havana, it stated that anyone from the Mississippi delta region could attend the university for free because the waters of the Mississippi touched the shores of Havana.

With the territory under the Spanish Crown, the Catholic Church in New Orleans fell under the jurisdiction of the Bishop of Santiago in Cuba. With the establishment of a diocese in Havana in 1787, the Cuban-born Auxiliary Bishop in New Orleans reported to the Bishop of Havana. Later, in 1799, the Diocese of Louisiana and the Floridas was established, and two years later the Cuban-born Luis Ignacio de Peñalver y Cárdenas became the first Bishop of Louisiana. The relationship was aided by proximity, and was a two way street. By the beginning of the 1800s, a boat departed New Orleans for Havana about every other day, carrying goods and people. One outcome of this relationship was the founding of the Cuban town of Cienfuegos in 1829 by the Clouet de Pierre y Favrot family of Louisiana.

When Louisiana came under American jurisdiction just after the turn of the nineteenth century, it became a center of independence efforts, not only for Cuba but for other Spanish colonies. Simón Bolívar spent time plotting his campaigns to free South America in the French Quarter, and later Beníto Júarez came there to plot to free Mexico from Maximillian's grasp. In 1850 and 1851 the Venezuelan-born Narciso López departed from New Orleans at the head of expeditions to free Cuba from Spain. López's altruistic pretensions were, however, overshadowed by his support for slavery and annexationist intentions. One of the more lasting outcomes of this period was the design in New Orleans for what later would become the Cuban flag.

Cuba's most respected patriot, José Martí, also spent time in New Orleans, in 1893 and 1894. Communication with the island was easy, as mail and passenger boats departed frequently. Not only did commerce flourish between the cities, but so did the arts. Dance troupes, theater and opera companies frequently traveled the 610-mile route between the cities. The shared history is evident in a walk through the French Quarter, which in its present form was principally built under the Spanish. With the aid of several *mojitos*, it could easily be confused with parts of old Havana. Both New Orleans and Havana are regularly battered by hurricanes, eaten by termites, and besieged by mosquitoes. In 1958, the year before the revolution, over six thousand people in New Orleans had jobs associated with trade with Cuba. In fact, Cuba was the single largest trading partner of the Port of New Orleans, accounting for over one third of all trade passing through the port. The history shared by Havana and New Orleans has made them quite natural sister cities.

New Orleans is, then, an excellent place to develop projects with

Cuba. One of the positive things about doing work with Cuba is that so many people from totally diverse backgrounds intersect on their interest in the island. One minute you can be talking to a musician with an interest in salsa, and the next to a bank executive wondering about future heavy machinery needs there. People who would not otherwise gather, do so because of a shared interest which previously did not find much expression. Just as I had been building my network of friends and associates in Cuba, I had been doing the same at home. Talks, musical performances, conferences, delegations and other outreach programs helped build a solid constituency of supporters in the city.

So, while organizing the congressional delegation, I was simultaneously organizing a cultural one of New Orleanians. In November of 1998 I again went to D.C. to meet with the Cuban mission and go over, in great detail, the itinerary for a cultural group. The visits to the mission were always odd affairs. A beautiful early twentieth-century building very much like many of the nicer houses in Havana of the same period, it has been kept up pretty well. What they lack in furniture they make up for in the aroma of tobacco. That day, no sooner had I put down my briefcase than they offered me a tour of the building. Climbing up the stairs, I mentally checked the documents I had brought, just in case I had anything there that they would find interesting. Returning several minutes later to the same room, I noticed my portfolio was still there, at a slightly different angle, and that a second door to the room that had previously been closed was now ajar.

After our discussions we agreed that the delegation would have about 35 members and would include musicians, whom it was agreed would perform in public, and civic and business leaders. They agreed to set up several meetings for the delegation, as well as to attend to some other details, such as visas. For the previous several months, I had also been planning an exhibit of photographs of New Orleans, confirming with our host, the University of Havana, the dates, place, time, etc. Things looked all set to go, and the delegation would attend the opening.

The proper process of securing visas to enter Cuba for the delegation wasn't much easier than working with my colleagues at the University of Havana. Our visas were supposed to be issued by the Cuban Interests Section in Washington, D.C. The folks making the air reservations can issue tourist visas, and it is no problem to enter the country with them no matter if you are a student, delegate or journalist — as long as you call yourself a tourist. Still, we were trying to play by the rules, and the routine usually went as follows: Just as with the university and their travel providers, we would send the required information to the Cuban Interests Section weeks, sometimes months, ahead of time. We would follow up, and be told that the names were being "analyzed," that is, sent through the Cuban intelligence database to see if there were any known spies or counterrevolutionaries among us. As the day of departure drew near, our follow-up calls became more frequent and importuning. At this point, the Cuban Interests Section would often claim that they had never received the list, an assertion easily countered by an express mail receipt. More time would pass, and usually just as it became clear that they would not be able to get us the visas in time, they would tell us to go ahead and just get tourist visas in Cancun. It was like a dog chasing its tail. In this case we were lucky, and I collected the visas for the delegation at the express mail facility on the way to the airport.

The timing of the event was both perfect and disastrous. A few days before we were to leave, the U.S. government announced a change of policy towards Cuba, which included the encouragement of cultural groups such as ours. Thus, we were on the leading edge of foreign policy. But there is always heat on the leading edge, and whatever the U.S. does, the Cuban government must make a big show of rejecting. So, on our arrival, the University of Havana claimed that they knew nothing of this exhibit, that it had never been approved or agreed to, and that not only would they not show the photographs, but had no plans to receive the delegation. Finally, after days of negotiation, they agreed to a very brief and private ceremony in which we would formally deliver the photos.

The New Orleans delegation was a diverse group. Over thirty strong, included Cuban Americans working in the mayor's office, trade and aviation representatives, business people, behind-the-scenes politicos, artists, photographers and, of course, the Trombone Shorty Brass Band. Being from a city known for its appreciation of pleasure, the participants also knew how to have fun. Despite the early flight, the party had begun before the wheels lifted off the runway. The second leg of the trip, however, from Cancún to Havana, showed the bitter irony of U.S.–Cuban relations. Sitting next to me was a woman of late middle age from Tarpon Springs, Florida, going to visit relatives in Havana. The exhaustion, sadness and resignation in her eyes were impossible to conceal. Her nephew had recently tried to come to join her on inner tubes and had been lost in the waters below. We were flying to the place he had fled.

As in almost any place with a rich history and open culture, just about everyone can find something they like in Havana. It is always amusing to see people on their first trip: they are totally fascinated, soaking it in through the same pores that they are soaking out of. What they don't realize is that while it is a deep culture, Cuba is in many ways like a small town.

You get a feel for it pretty quickly. But then again, it is in many ways a very sensuous place, and it is hard to tire of that.

I might as well have crumpled up the itinerary back home. I would have been glad if, as with the congressional group, official Cuba had stuck some new program in my hands when we got off the plane. Instead, they simply stood us up for every meeting and every event that they had agreed to. It reminded me of when I once let the wind unspool a kite line, only to find out that it was not tied at the end. There is a certain feeling when one sees a kite, unbridled, gently swaying in the wind as it slowly makes its way back to earth, far out of reach. There was not much I could do. I met with the people at the university, and after keeping me waiting in a hall for two hours like a miscreant schoolboy, they went on indignantly insisting how they knew nothing about this, lying the entire time.

Gathering our delegation, we headed to the bus at the appointed hour to formally hand over the photographs. At first, there was some delay in entering the university, but after about fifteen minutes we were allowed in. At night in a small, dimly lit courtyard, they had placed a few photos on some overturned cardboard boxes. Here we gathered with about ten university officials, and said a few nice words about the historical and cultural links which we shared. They let it be known that this was to be a brief ceremony, and it was devoid of the usual flowery language employed during such occasions. Once the talking was over, the band began to play. But after only a few tunes, the director of international relations, who a couple of years earlier had educated me so thoroughly on the history of the university, now curtly explained that the music was disturbing students who were studying. He apparently feared that some students might be attracted by the music. We did manage to have a few pictures taken, next to a tank kept on the university plaza.

The people in the delegation were very easygoing, and were probably just as glad not to have a bunch of meetings to go to. The one event we did not need Cuban government participation in was the planned jazz parade through Old Havana. The next afternoon, we loaded ourselves, and our drinks, onto the bus and headed towards the old Plaza de Armas. Armed only with our instruments and some Mardi Gras throws to give away, we deployed in the square. Our band struck up, the music from trumpets, tuba, drums and tambourines ricocheting through the narrow colonial streets as our "second line" parade marched forward. A crowd quickly gathered, dancing to the music and reaching for beads, doubloons and balls as if it they were edible.

Soon, the notorious "black berets" decided that things had gone too far. Recall that these are provincial toughs brought in to keep the

Habaneros in line, and are even resented by the local police. They stop just about everybody they can whistle at, and those they decide are out of line they load up in military transport trucks for interrogation and detention. Well, we certainly were out of line, and after repeated efforts, they forced the band to stop playing. Retreating to a nearby open-air restaurant, we refreshed our drinks, and the band began a jam session with the restaurant band. Soon the same crowd pressed against the railing and everyone, inside and out, was gyrating to the rhythm. A couple of *mojitos* later, I decided that we should continue our jazz crusade to the Cathedral Square, where our bus was waiting nearby. I asked our tuba player, a gentle man who looks like Isaac Hayes' big brother, to play and march, and if anyone tried to stop him, especially if he had a black beret on, to keep marching. No one in their right mind would stand in front of this guy.

The band struck up again, and the party, now bigger than ever, took to the streets, people joining as we went along. Unable to pass a bar without refreshing ourselves, we stormed the Café Paris, despite the desperate, lone efforts of the doorman to stem the crowd which flowed in like water through a burst dam. A few tunes and a fresh drink later, we continued on our last leg towards the square. By now the black berets had given up trying to stop us, and were escorting us, just like the parades back home, and the crowd continued their revellion in the streets. Celebrating our arrival at the square, we continued to treat our new friends, and the ever-larger contingent of black berets, to the beats of a music that their country had helped to develop.

By now it was dinner-time. I had made arrangements at La Guarida, a local paladar, for our group. The only difficulty in leaving was that someone had fallen in love with one of the musicians, and it was only with wails and tears that she could be pried from her new love. La Guarida is without question one of the best private restaurants in Cuba, and the quality of their food is complemented by a relaxed, bohemian atmosphere. In Spanish, "*guarida*" refers to a hideout, and it was a hideout that we really needed right then. Once there, stepping on the third floor balcony, I looked out to see at least a dozen black berets in perimeter formation below. It would not have served them to arrest us, especially as the Cuban Interests Section had approved the event, and taking a lesson from U.S. Cold War policy, they decided that the best policy was containment. Dinner for over thirty in a small restaurant takes a bit of time. After an hour or so, alcohol alone could no longer stave off the hunger, though not for lack of trying. Taking the lead yet again, to the astonishment of the cooks, our tuba player entered the kitchen, announced he was too hungry to wait any longer, donned an apron and set about preparing his own meal. Finally the rest of us ate, and straggled past the cordon of black berets back to the bus and to the hotel. The official Cubans were quite unhappy over all this, but the Cuban people did not mind, in fact those that attended were ecstatic over the parade, and rumors circulated for quite some time that another one was imminent.

CHAPTER 6

Cubans in Exile and the Monistic Legacy

Overall, despite the obstacles, the cultural delegation had been a success: The participants had gotten what they wanted, if not exactly what they had come for; in New Orleans the right-wing monopoly of silence on Cuba was in pieces; and there was now going to be a real discussion concerning our relationship with Cuba. All of the major local constituencies were now engaged: the arts, business, political, and academic communities. It was almost a Phyrric victory, though, as the Cuban government, and their mission in D.C., were not in a talkative mood. I wondered if I would ever be able to go back to Cuba, or even to run the summer program down there any more. Security to them is always first, but money is a close second, and they are constantly trying to balance the two. In the end, I did return and the summer program continued to grow.

Back home, as is so often the case after trips to Cuba, a lot of people laid low. Part of it is that it was always an exhausting trip, but, in New Orleans at least, some of the participants would face criticism for going. This was not the case with Jim Varney, the *Times-Picayune* reporter on the trip. He and his paper have always been friends of greater contact with Cuba and gave us a good front-page story and two banner-headed pages inside. As we will see, others on the trip lacked *The Picayune*'s courage.

The reader must recognize by this point that I am far from romanticizing what is and has been happening on the island. Castro is a tyrant, a despot. He has distorted and prostituted the ideals of the revolution of 1959 for the sake of his own ego, and holds a nation hostage to a brittle and failed vision. Far worse, Castro has denied his people the exercise of freedom of speech, association, and travel, and the right to determine their future.

These accusations are what the dominant voices of the Cuban American community say, and I agree with those accusations. Furthermore, I sympathize with those who make the accusations. Although some of them, or their parents, may have abused their fellow citizens before 1959, most have lost their ability to live in the land of their birth and lost their property through the type of expropriation that has aggrieved and wounded so many in the twentieth century. Were I a Cuban living in exile in Miami or anywhere else, I would feel much the same anger, the same bitterness, the same desire for revenge, the same injustice that so many Cuban Americans do. So why is it that my and Tulane's Cuban Studies Institute's principal opposition in New Orleans came from the leadership of the Cuban American community? To understand that, one must know something about that group and its leaders.

The Cuban American community is splintered by many divisions. That should come as no surprise if you have spent much time in Cuba. Two main fault lines among the exiles, however, are class and generation. Many Cubans who immigrated immediately after the revolution were from the upper classes. Take a trip down many Havana streets and you will see the graceful and elegant mansions that they lost. As time went on, the social origins of the immigrants became more humble, perhaps best exemplified by the Mariel exodus of 1980. Some of those people had been members of the pre-revolutionary middle and working classes, though many others were younger and had only known revolutionary Cuba; and some were criminals Castro threw in to rid himself of a problem and cause one for the U.S.

Emigration has always been a good escape valve for the most discontented, and as a result the U.S. got not only many of the brightest, but also many of the angriest Cuba had to offer. Many Cuban Americans still resent the abuses visited upon them under Batista, and the many benefits the former ruling class— and first wave of immigrants— gained from that system. To some, the elitist leadership of the conservative Cuban American community is conducting a war for themselves, seeking to regain their previous privileges back home. Some of the later immigrants supported the revolution initially; Castro based his appeal to the middle and working classes on the restoration of the nation's 1940 constitution, a document which was not unlike ours. Had he not won over the middle classes, he probably never would have achieved power. Castro's true colors did not fully come out until he was safely ensconced as head of Cuba's government

The other fault line is generational. The Cubans who came over in the sixties are old-timers now, and their children and grandchildren are naturally curious about the island. If Americans suffer from a desire to taste the forbidden fruit, then many second-and-third generation Cuban Americans are positively ravenous. Its proximity and a continuing influx of new migrants only whets the appetite further. This group grew up listening to stories of back home, how beautiful the island is, how this evil man has taken away what should have been their inheritance, how millions are held hostage. It is not that they support Castro, nor that they necessarily want to rebel against their parents, just that, like so many Americans, they want to see it for themselves, they want to form their own opinions. It is such a part of their identity, but at the same time a void, that they want to put substance where there have been only words and the experiences of others.

The problem is that to do this, many of these young people must suffer the everlasting condemnation of their parents and many of their relatives. To say they want to go to Cuba is like a son of orthodox Jews coming home and announcing that he is marrying a Muslim. It is anathema. I have received letters from second-generation Cuban Americans, telling me how happy they are that an academic program exists, telling me how much they want to go on it, and confiding that if their parents knew they were even writing the letter they would not forgive them. On the whole, the second generation is much more open- minded and very pleasant to deal with. Those who have gone to Cuba generally get the most out of it, though there are those who lack discretion and feel that it is incumbent on them to start a revolution in their brief time there.

Just as the conservatives are spread over generations, so are the moderates. They have to contend with a small, privileged group of extremists who jealously dominate the political landscape, and speak not only for all Cuban Americans, but for all Cubans as well. It is just like back home. Those who disagree with their heavy-handed ways and extremist positions are branded sympathizers, or worse, communists. If they see that you are going to go to Cuba over their objections, they try to guide you as an evangelical might try to guide one away from idolatry. They patronizingly suggest that you meet with the dissidents, that you get away from your handlers in Cuba and "talk to the people, see what they have to say." The presumption is that one has a handler in Cuba, which most people who travel there independently don't, and that you would not do this anyway. Their worldview, and sometimes their methods, hark back to the chilling, sordid days of the McCarthy era. Accusation of slander is another dagger that is rarely kept in its sheath, and legal actions against people who say things about these extremist Cuban Americans that they do not like seek not only to silence those who differ with them, but also to give pause to others who may object to their views and ways.

Combined with this is a near-total disconnect from reality. Many of the conservative Cuban American leaders live in an echo chamber of their own making. Many haven't been to Cuba in forty-plus years. Although they see photos and talk to relatives and others on the phone, they have lost the feel for the place. One of the things they fail to recognize is that the conservatives are thoroughly resented in Cuba by ordinary Cubans. It is one of the many ironies of the place. Almost every Cuban on the island has at least one relative in the U.S., often Miami or Union City, New Jersey, whom they love. But this individual relationship is not to be confused with their collective relationship to Miami. To them "Miami" is the reason there is an embargo, and when Castro dies and the whole thing comes crashing down it will be "Miami" that will be borne across the straits, the tattered and yellowed sails of their land deeds filled with the wind of their vitriol, coming home to reclaim what was theirs perhaps half a century ago. And, of course, Castro knows all this, and plays it like a virtuoso, heightening fears on the island of an arrogant mob tossing people out into the streets while at the same time apparently doing a fairly good job of maintaining his intelligence apparatus in Miami. The latter sends home information that sows further distrust, discord and rancor among the community — something easily done: Castro has been the winner of the game the entire time, in no small part because everyone plays it.

This group, the extreme Right of the immigrant Cuban community are perhaps better called "Cuban Not So Americans." Like Cubans at a rally pretending to be communists, they pretend to be American but have little tolerance of differing ideas or genuine understanding of civil liberties. Many only came for a few months, over forty years ago. And unlike almost any other immigrant group, they have spent their entire time here trying to go home. Almost all immigrants to America came fleeing something, and most in a fairly short time stopped looking back. The Cuban Right has done nothing but look back; America is not a home, but rather just a port in a storm that lasted longer than expected. Ironically, they are neither appreciated, eagerly awaited, nor, en masse, welcome back home. Many are so disconnected from the reality in Cuba that they don't realize this is the case.

The saddest thing about the Cuban American right wing is that they give a bad name to Cuban Americans generally. Like Castro, they have arrogated unto themselves the right to speak for others. This is what the Cuban Americans came here to escape, and yet their own people continue to do it to them. There are many Cuban Americans who are moderate and promote dialogue, but they are shouted down or quietly pressured by the old line Right. They also lack the financial resources, and the extensive political influence that money can buy, to effectively compete against the extreme right. The problem is with a small, vocal, often wealthy and well-organized group — angry toughs who act more like a Mafia than Americans. It is a cross that the rest of the Cuban Americans unjustly bear. It also underscores the resiliency of the monistic impulse in Cuban culture, which life in America has done little to change.

The Right claims to be fighting for liberty and democracy in Cuba. Given the history of their actions in the U.S., this is open to a lot of doubt. Threats, violence, extortion and social ostracism for those who hold different views is not the stuff of which democracy is made. It is, in fact, the stuff of which Castro's system is made. In an April 2000, article entitled "The Burden of a Violent History," in the *Miami New Times* , Jim Mullin catalogued a series of violent incidents attributed to the Cuban American Right in Miami. Some of them follow in this excerpt*:

> You know you've got image problems when the staid New York Times editorializes with evident concern that it appears "as if South Florida's Cuban Americans believe in mob rule."
>
> Lawless violence and intimidation have been hallmarks of el exilio for more than 30 years. Given that fact, it's not only understandable many people would be deeply worried, it's prudent to be worried. Of course it goes without saying that the majority of Cuban Americans in Miami do not sanction violence, but its long tradition within the exile community cannot be ignored and cannot simply be wished away.
>
> The following list of violent incidents I compiled from a variety of databases and news sources (a few come from personal experience). It is incomplete, especially in Miami's trademark category of bomb threats. Nor does it include dozens of acts of violence and murder committed by Cuban exiles in other U.S. cities and at least sixteen foreign countries. But completeness isn't the point. The point is to face the truth, no matter how difficult that may be. If Miami's Cuban exiles confront this shameful past — and resolutely disavow it — they will go a long way toward easing their neighbors' anxiety about a peaceful future.
>
> 1968   From MacArthur Causeway, pediatrician Orlando Bosch fires bazooka at a Polish freighter. (City of Miami later declares "Orlando Bosch Day." Federal agents will jail him in 1988.)
>
> 1972   Julio Iglesias, performing at a local nightclub, says he wouldn't mind "singing in front of Cubans." Audience erupts in anger. Singer requires police escort. Most radio stations drop Iglesias from playlists. One that doesn't, Radio Alegre, receives bomb threats.
>
> 1974   Bomb blast guts the office of Spanish-language magazine *Replica.*
>
> 1974   Several small Cuban businesses, citing threats, stop selling *Replica.*

1974   Three bombs explode near a Spanish-language radio station.

1974   Hector Diaz Limonta and Arturo Rodriguez Vives murdered in internecine exile power struggles.

1975   Luciano Nieves murdered after advocating peaceful coexistence with Cuba.

1975   Another bomb damages *Replica*'s office.

1976   Rolando Masferrer and Ramon Donestevez murdered in internecine exile power struggles.

1976   Car bomb blows off legs of WQBA-AM news director Emilio Milian after he publicly condemns exile violence.

1977   Juan José Peruyero murdered in internecine exile power struggles.

1979   Cuban film "Memories of Underdevelopment" interrupted by gunfire and physical violence instigated by two exile groups.

1979   Bomb discovered at Padron Cigars, whose owner helped negotiate release of 3600 Cuban political prisoners.

1979   Bomb explodes at Padron Cigars.

1980   Another bomb explodes at Padron Cigars.

1980   Powerful anti-personnel bomb discovered at American Airways Charter, which arranges flights to Cuba.

1981   Bomb explodes at Mexican Consulate on Brickell Avenue in protest of relations with Cuba.

1981   *Replica*'s office again damaged by a bomb.

1982   Two outlets of Hispania Interamericana, which ships medicine to Cuba, attacked by gunfire.

1982   Bomb explodes at Venezuelan Consulate in downtown Miami in protest of relations with Cuba.

1982   Miami Mayor Maurice Ferre defends $10,000 grant to exile commando group Alpha 66 by noting that the organization "has never been accused of terrorist activities inside the United States."

1983   Another bomb discovered at Replica.

1983   Another bomb explodes at Padron Cigars.

1983   Bomb explodes at Paradise International, which arranges travel to Cuba.

1983   Bomb explodes at Little Havana office of Continental National Bank, one of whose executives, Bernardo Benes, helped negotiate release of 3600 Cuban political prisoners.

1983   Miami City Commissioner Demetrio Perez seeks to honor exile terrorist Juan Felipe de la Cruz, accidentally killed while assembling a bomb.

1983   Gunfire shatters windows of three Little Havana businesses linked to Cuba.

1987   Bomb explodes at Cuba Envios, which ships packages to Cuba.

1987   Bomb explodes at Almacen El Español, which ships packages to Cuba.

1987   Bomb explodes at Cubanacan, which ships packages to Cuba.

1987   Bomb explodes at Machi Viajes a Cuba, which arranges travel to Cuba.

1987   Bomb explodes outside Va Cuba, which ships packages to Cuba.
1988   Bomb explodes at Miami Cuba, which ships medical supplies to Cuba.
1988   Bomb threat against Iberia Airlines in protest of Spain's relations with Cuba.
1988   Bomb explodes outside Cuban Museum of Art and Culture after auction of paintings by Cuban artists.
1988   Bomb explodes outside home of Maria Cristina Herrera, organizer of a conference on U.S.-Cuba relations.
1988   Bomb threat against WQBA-AM after commentator denounces Herrera bombing.
1988   Bomb threat at local office of Immigration and Naturalization Service in protest of terrorist Orlando Bosch being jailed.
1988   Bomb explodes near home of Griselda Hidalgo, advocate of unrestricted travel to Cuba.
1988   Bomb damages Bele Cuba Express, which ships packages to Cuba.
1989   Another bomb discovered at Almacen El Español, which ships packages to Cuba.
1989   Two bombs explode at Marazul Charters, which arranges travel to Cuba.
1990   Another, more powerful, bomb explodes outside the Cuban Museum of Art and Culture.
1991   Using crowbars and hammers, exile crowd rips out and urinates on Calle Ocho "Walk of Fame" star of Mexican actress Veronica Castro, who had visited Cuba.
1992   Union Radio employee beaten and station vandalized by exiles looking for Francisco Aruca, who advocates an end to U.S. embargo.
1992   Americas Watch releases report stating that hard-line Miami exiles have created an environment in which "moderation can be a dangerous position."
1993   Inflamed by Radio Mambí commentator Armando Perez-Roura, Cuban exiles physically assault demonstrators lawfully protesting against U.S. embargo.
1994   Human Rights Watch/Americas Group issues report stating that Miami exiles do not tolerate dissident opinions, that Spanish-language radio promotes aggression, and that local government leaders refuse to denounce acts of intimidation.
1994   Two firebombs explode at Replica magazine's office.
1994   Bomb threat to law office of Magda Montiel Davis following her videotaped exchange with Fidel Castro.
1996   Music promoter receives threatening calls, cancels local appearance of Cuba's La Orquesta Aragon.
1996   Patrons attending concert by Cuban jazz pianist Gonzalo Rubalcaba physically assaulted by 200 exile protesters. Transportation for exiles arranged by Dade County Commissioner Javier Souto.
1996   Firebomb explodes at Little Havana's Centro Vasco restaurant preceding concert by Cuban singer Rosita Fornes.

1996   Firebomb explodes at Marazul Charters, which arranges travel to Cuba.

1996   Arson committed at Tu Familia Shipping, which ships packages to Cuba.

1997   Bomb threats, death threats received by radio station WRTO-FM following its short-lived decision to include in its playlist songs by Cuban musicians.

1998   Bomb threat empties concert hall at MIDEM music conference during performance by 91-year-old Cuban musician Compay Segundo.

1998   Bomb threat received by Amnesia nightclub in Miami Beach preceding performance by Cuban musician Orlando "Maraca" Valle.

1998   Firebomb explodes at Amnesia nightclub preceding performance by Cuban singer Manolín.

1999   Violent protest at Miami Arena performance of Cuban band Los Van Van leaves one person injured, eleven arrested.

1999 Bomb threat received by Seville Hotel in Miami Beach preceding performance by Cuban singer Rosita Fornes. Hotel cancels concert.

January 26, 2000   Outside Miami Beach home of Sister Jeanne O'Laughlin, protester displays sign reading, "Stop the deaths at sea. Repeal the Cuban Adjustment Act," then is physically assaulted by nearby exile crowd before police come to rescue.

April 11, 2000   Outside home of Elian Gonzalez's Miami relatives, radio talk show host Scot Piasant of Portland, Oregon, displays T-shirt reading, "Send the boy home" and "A father's rights," then is physically assaulted by nearby exile crowd before police come to rescue.*

The worst part of the hypocrisy of the Cuban American Right concerns money. Many charge that academic and cultural programs only put money in Castro's hands, helping him to oppress the masses. The fact is that very little money comes into his hands that way, perhaps a quarter to a half a million dollars from all the academic and cultural programs combined. But where does Castro get his money? Tourism is the leading sector now, netting two or three hundred million dollars a year. Mineral extraction, especially of nickel, gives about the same. Sugar is a basket case, the Siberia of ministry appointments, and loses money, all the more after Hurricane Michelle in 2001.

The single largest source of hard currency for Cuba — and for Castro — comes from where you would least expect it: the Cuban American community. A United Nations study put the figure at about six hundred to eight hundred million dollars annually from the exile community. This does not include the value of care packages, and is more than double the

*Jim Mullin, "The Burden of a Violent History," Miami New Times, April 20, 2000. Reprinted with permission.

net from tourism, and perhaps more than tourism and mining combined. And remittances are pure cash; there is no overhead. It is the Cuban Americans who are financing Castro, it is them he looks to, gazing serenely across the straits, when he wonders where Cuba's next dollar is coming from. It is the Cuban American Right that supports squeezing the Cuban government (and people) with the embargo, yet they continue to send their money to Cuba. I asked an exile leader once about this curious hole in their logic, and he indignantly protested that it was for relatives, not for Castro. But, just as the same person had told me so many times before, with very few exceptions it ends up in the hands of the state.

The Right have consistently promoted their own interests over America's national interest, and over the interests of Cuba. Money from Cuban Americans does not only go to Havana, it also goes to Washington. American policy towards Cuba is the product of a complex of factors, of which the Cuban American Right are an important but not the only part. Their extensive funding of political campaigns, and the threat of funding opposition campaigns, is a major reason that the policy towards Cuba has changed so little in more than forty years. Seeking to explain why we trade with China and Vietnam and not Cuba, many in Congress have learned the "trade two step." Once, asked to give a reason why we should trade with China, someone responded that there were over a billion reasons to trade there. Senator Trent Lott offered two more. Appearing on Fox News Sunday (5/30/00), he argued that we should trade with China because it is the best way we have of controlling their behavior, and because they already have access to our economy. He rejected trade with Cuba, however, because Castro hates the U.S. and is more "vicious" because he killed two Cuban Americans in the shootdown of a Brothers to the Rescue aircraft in 1996. On the one hand, he is correct that engagement does give us more leverage than isolation. The argument that the Chinese already have access to our markets is weak, however, suggesting that the Chinese government has given the U.S. a fait accompli and that we have no control over whom we trade with. No human life is worth more than any other, but the Chinese government has jailed and killed a lot more people than Castro. Yet, according to Senator Lott, they are not as vicious.

The whole thing revolves around money. China is big, and big business has lots invested there, and would be upset with Lott's re-election campaign if he did anything to limit their opportunities there. Cuba is a relatively small market, although big business would like to have access to it. But most on Capitol Hill prefer to play it safe and follow the path of contradiction lest the Cuban American Right lavish funds on their opponents.

It is interesting to listen to representatives expound on the virtues of free trade, how the need for information demanded by commerce pries open closed societies, how people subsequently absorb the values of developed countries and how once you introduce economic accountability through the market the same inevitably, even if slowly, will happen with the government. Then they talk about Cuba and insist that it is a "special case," that unlike other countries, we need to tighten the screws on Castro. The only consistency is inconsistency. But many on the Hill do recognize that our interests are not served by the present policy and would like to see a fresh approach after all of these years. They recognize that the best way for them to promote this is to determine what the embargo is costing their constituency, and to help to disseminate this information.

Pedro Ortíz, the local chapter president of a right-wing Cuban American group in New Orleans, wasted no time in trying to exact revenge from those who had participated in the cultural delegation in 1998. I later understood that he called an executive of a local bank who had participated in the trip, telling him that he was going to order his followers to close their accounts if the bank did not make a public apology. Although Tulane University was a much larger depositer in the bank than the local Cuban American community, the bank sent a cowardly letter to the editor of the *Times-Picayune* distancing itself from the trip, apologizing for its participation, and expressing criticism of the Cuban government. Thus, the only large business that showed a vision of the future had now done a full and public grovel to the Cuban right.

My own first meeting with Ortíz was by phone, as word spread that we were organizing the first summer session in 1996. Hardly a syllable of the word Cuba could be mentioned in New Orleans without invoking his name. Originally, I thought that people respected him, but I was to learn that they just feared him. He had been "the man," squelching any thought of doing anything in Cuba, or about Cuba, or even exploring opportunities after Castro dies, for many years.

Bellowing into the phone, Ortíz announced that he was the President of a large Cuban American organization, and was outraged that I had taken students down to Cuba. I asked to be corrected, but wasn't Francisco Gómez the president of his organization? After some silence and then clearing of the throat, he said that he was in fact the president of the local chapter. I explained to him that we operated entirely within American laws, and that in fact we were implementing the very foreign policy that his organization spends so many thousands of dollars every year to influence. Anyway, students are entitled to form their own opinions, and I pointed out that we were an academic institution free to develop our programs. A pause. He then insisted that he be allowed to make a presentation to the students concerning the nature of Castro's police state. I explained that the U.S. Mission in Havana took care of that. He then demanded, at the least, that we distribute the literature of his organization. Strange as it sounded, this was not an entirely bad idea. Students should be free to make up their own minds. I said so, but added that it would not be possible as most of the students were not from New Orleans and would meet up in Cancún and it would not be prudent to enter Cuba with such literature. Thus began a relationship that despite my sincere efforts to find some middle ground, would result in Ortíz doing everything in his power to destroy the programs that I was developing.

Contrary to the Right's assertions, I made a point of presenting both sides of issues, often through speakers I would bring to the university. I was trying not only to be fair, but to generate discussion and dialogue. What the conservatives did not like was that I invited people to talk whom they did not agree with. I did invite their own to talk as well. In an unprecedented alliance, Ortíz and I organized a double header, having both a high-ranking member from his organization and a congresswoman from Florida on the same night. It was quite an event, and I publicized it like any other. There was a good crowd there, and all were delighted to see the guests. Usually, I leave the mingling until after the talk, but there was plenty of chitchat as the speakers made their way up to the dais. Ortíz wanted it that way, because "I know my people" and more would be coming. In the Latin tradition, I made a flowery and complimentary introduction noting Ortíz's leadership of many Cuban Americans and how much Cuban Americans have contributed to the United States. And then Ortíz made a similarly conciliatory speech. Things seemed to be going well.

The event soon took on a tone of a religious revival. The congresswoman was a bit cautious, restricting herself to lambasting attempts to erode the embargo in Congress, blasting Clinton for the tepid steps he had taken to promote the flow of information to the island (and to allow programs such as this to develop). For her, the nice thing about doing a double barrel program like this was that she could agree with what the other speaker had to say without saying it herself. Virtue by association. After hearty applause for the congresswoman, Ortíz introduced the other speaker, his eyes welling with tears as he recounted how he had helped carry his father's coffin, reveling in the leadership qualities of the young man who could certainly fill his father's shoes.

The official took the ball and ran, and in no time he was insisting that "we have already won," a totally baseless assertion which nonetheless prompted enthusiastic cheers and applause from the crowd. He went on, claiming that Castro is on his last legs (just as Castro says capitalism is at its end), that never before has the Cuban American community been so united (the opposite is in fact true), and that an uprising on the island was imminent (something else they have been saying for over forty years, though they will obviously not be the ones leading it). The crowd was wild: The prophet was before them, reassuring them that salvation was at hand.

There was only one student among the audience, someone who actually never had missed an event. We had publicized this talk as we had everything else: extensively. It seems that neither the students nor the general public had any interest in the revelations of the prophet. As usual, the question and answer period had as many speeches as questions, but there were some questions that stood out. One concerned how CNN was able to legally operate on the island. Instead of answering the question and explaining that they were licensed by the U.S. and Cuban governments, the prophet looked pained, and said that in Miami, they call it "Castro's News Network." He went on to explain that he thought it was shameful that they were allowed to operate there, and that if he had his way, they would not be there at all. I was amazed that he would actually call for the end of the freedom of the press. The crowd applauded his view.

Before long, the questions started to shift to me. One, saying that he had read in the paper that I had said that students were in Cuba to learn about democracy, asked how could that be so? Before I could begin to answer that, another blurted out that she thought it was terrible that I took students to Cuba, and asked, how could I do that to them? I responded in turn, explaining that not only did I choose my words carefully, but that I kept a close tab on what was written in the papers about the program. I suggested that the gentleman reread the article, because I had never said such a thing. I added that despite that, the students did learn quite a bit about democracy in Cuba, noting that one of the best ways to understand how something works is to take out critical components.

In Cuba, that is done for you, and after a few weeks there people understand just how important is a free press, the right to associate, to express oneself and to choose and hold your leaders accountable. In fact, Cuba is an excellent place to learn about how democracy works, by seeing how its opposite doesn't. To the second question, I said that while I respected the fact that she did not think it was appropriate to send students to Cuba, it was their decision to make, not hers. I pointed out that all of the students were adults, and not only were capable but had the right to form and hold their own opinions. Furthermore, it was the responsibility of the university to provide students with opportunities to see and experience social, cultural and political systems different than their own.

In the end, "backpack diplomacy" was one of the factors credited with bringing down the Soviet Union.

At the end of the meeting, when I was thanking the speakers for coming to Tulane, I noticed a short but muscular man in his sixties standing to the side. As I walked away he came up to me, blocking my path, and standing forward, his chin extended, he said "Castro killed my son, and you are an accomplice to his murder. I will remember your face," and turned abruptly away. No harm ever came to me, however, and no violence against my person or property was ever committed. It was, nevertheless, an act of attempted intimidation.

I knew that there was a tremendous, repressed interest in Cuba among the business community in New Orleans, and wanted to tap it. The World Trade Center, of which I was a member, agreed to co-sponsor a luncheon examining post-embargo trade opportunities in Cuba. The conference was about trading with Cuba not now, but at some time in the future when it would be legal. The announcements were sent out and the reservations streamed in. As a board member of the group, Ortíz heard about it and lost no time in organizing his forces to try to squash the whole thing. He lobbied the board and bullied the organization's director, a kind man who has many virtues, one of which is as a consensus builder. Ortíz attacked the person I had invited, the nation's foremost expert on the Cuban economy and trade opportunities, accusing him of misrepresenting what some large corporations had said concerning their interest in Cuba. The board was now agitated, and the director, on the run, wanted out. I reminded him that he knew from the beginning that there would be some heat for this, which at the time he recognized and did not see as a problem. I pointed out that we would both lose credibility if he canceled, and, most importantly, that Ortíz should not be the one deciding what people hear. He refused to honor the original agreement, and wanted to change it to a panel and put some conservative Cuban Americans on it. Ortíz was on a rampage, and I was told that he was calling me a communist and doing whatever he could to kill or eviscerate the event.

I wasn't worried about the possibility of cancellation, as I had a backup plan. What I wanted was to demonstrate that people could gather to rationally explore what the future economic potential of Cuba would be, under the aegis of a trade group. As a member, I could reserve a room and hold an event. The event was already announced, and all that would have been necessary would be to change the name under which the room was reserved. But I did not suggest this; I did not want to give them an out. I had a choice, was it more important to go it alone, or to do the event in conjunction with the trade group? Even if it was debased, I felt that it would still be a step forward if the group were to be involved. I agreed to have one of the conservative Cuban Americans on board.

On the day of the event, I learned Ortíz was still trying to prevent me from making welcoming remarks, claiming that I was not a neutral party. To some extent this was true: I wanted people to think about post-embargo trade and I did and do think that trade is good and would undermine the Castro government. I refused to distance myself from the meeting I had organized and fought for, and if they wanted to cancel the whole thing over it, so be it. I had proposed it, had brought the main attraction, and I was going to introduce him. My guest noted that never had he seen such opposition for a talk. But the hour came, and the people flowed in not only from New Orleans but from neighboring states as well, and the event not only went smoothly, but was a tremendous success. I was later told that not in almost half a century had any luncheon on foreign trade had such a turnout. Even Chango, the Santería orisha of fire, lightning and war that Felipe had told me was my guardian spirit, attended, ending a long drought and visiting many lightning bolts on the roof just overhead. Ortíz had been defeated in his own lair.

In a follow-up survey sent to participants, the only criticism several expressed was the participation of the Cuban American rightist. It seemed that no one was interested in what he had to say. The people had spoken; the event showed that there was tremendous interest in trade with Cuba, and that it was possible to explore it. The monologue of the Cuban American Right had become a debate. It also widened the base of support for my work, and would serve as a springboard for future endeavors.

Having tried to stop us at every step, and having failed to cancel any project, Ortíz and his followers decided to try a new strategy. Instead of trying to cancel events, they would try to have the Cuban Studies Institute abolished. The university president, Eamon Kelly, who, along with Vice-President William Bertrand, had been so helpful in establishing the program, had in the intervening time resigned, and it was not clear where the new president, Scott Cowen, stood on the issue. I had tried for some time to get an appointment to brief him on the complex political landscape of Tulane in Cuba. He had just assumed office, however, and so was focused on other issues. A board member had requested that Cowen receive Ortíz and a Cuban American member of the medical school faculty. This he did, and I understood that in their meeting with him they told him we were brainwashing students and that the Cuban American community opposed the programs. They asked him, a Jew, if he would support a study-abroad program in Nazi Germany, and they said we did not give time for both sides. They demanded that the institute be permanently closed. Given their track record I would not have been surprised if they had accused me of being a communist, and threatened to start a campaign to ask university donors not to give to the institution. I had been told by the chair of another department that they had threatened his program with a cutoff of contributions in retaliation for the activities of the Cuban Studies Institute. What I did know, and they did not, was that despite being affable, President Cowen does not like it when people try to twist his arm.

The day following their meeting, President Cowen found time for me on his schedule. He invited me in and allowed me to respond to the accusations. Soon, it became clear that letting me defend myself was only part of the reason I was there; the other was that he wanted to tell someone how peeved he was, how these guys had the gall to try to push him around. How he told the medical school professor that he was ashamed that he has so little appreciation of academic freedom that he would come to him and say these things. How rude and pushy these folks were. And how, in the end, the meeting was abruptly ended and he showed them the door. It was a relief, because now I had support for the program at the top, and just as importantly, the president knew what I was up against. Ortíz had done me the biggest favor he probably ever will.

Some of my contacts with "the opposition" as I inevitably began to think of Ortíz and his followers, were not direct, but were by mail. Most were anonymous and critical of the institute's efforts. Let me quote two: the first from a student at Tulane, the second anonymous. I have not corrected spellings.

> To Whom It May Concern,
>
> I am a Cuban American student here at the university and I would like to express my concerns regarding the events and speakers organized by the Cuban Studies Institute.
>
> Almost every time I receive an email regarding an event being sponsered by the Cuban studies institute, I scroll down to find that all of these individuals are simpathetic and cooperative with the existing communist regime in Cuba. It upsets me greatly that we are painting such a one-sided and imcomplete picture of what Cuba is, of what Cuban culture and politics is, of the reality of a whole other group of people on the island.
>
> Now I'm not asking that the Cuban Studies Institute take side. Would one anti-revolutionary speaker be too much too much to ask. I was raised a Cuban, even though it was in the United States. I consider myself very much Cuban in everyway, but yet I do not feel represented by the speakers or events that you sponser. I can guarantee you that my Cuban parents wouldn't either. So, if there is a whole section of Cubans that aren't being represented by your institute's programming, then how can it truly be a Cuban Studies Institute? Wouldn't that just make it a Communist Cuban

studies instiitute, since that's all we are presenting. You are presenting an inaccurate picture of Cubans and Cuban life by not balancing out your program. Many Americans who attend these programs frequently aren't aware of the injustices that have indeniably occurred and continue to occur in Cuba.

We take for granted all the opportunities we're blessed with in Our country. For anyone who tells me that this is not true, I challenge you to spend some time on the other side of Cuba. Not the side where you can stay in tourist hotels, eat at tourist restaurant, relax at tourist beaches and never notice the world outside your little block, but the side with sinking houses and half demolished buildings, and long food lines, and fear.

It is saddening to think that I cannot be comfortable with and proud of something that is supposed to study "Cubans". I am very dissappointed and I know that I am not the only one. I hope that these considerations will be taken into account and that perhaps there would be some changes in the institute's programming.

Sincerely,
XXX

This letter says a great deal. First there is the false accusation that different views are not presented. I don't know why, but people tend to line up to listen to people they hate. Apparently, he didn't care to attend a panel of former political prisoners, of Cuban American conservatives, or the numerous U.S. government officials that gave talks. Also, it shows a lack of understanding of how things work in Cuba to complain that visitors from the island are cooperative with the government. Regrettably, in Cuba, just about everyone works for the government. Also regrettably, Castro is not going to let dissidents out for a university speaking tour. Cuba is a despotism, and those who are permitted to speak publicly abroad, the " exit visa elite," will say they support the government. What is most telling in the letter, however, is that the writer confesses that he was "raised a Cuban" and feels "very much Cuban in every way." That is precisely the problem: American political culture has not rubbed off on him nor, apparently, his family. The democratic virtues of tolerance and respect for those with whom one disagrees are not part of his worldview. Those whom he does not agree with, from ignorance or for any other reason, must be communists or communist dupes, and hence the Institute is communist. Finally, it is indicative of the conceit of many that he would "challenge you to spend some time on the other side of Cuba," something apparently the student never had done. Naturally, the assumption is that students and others manage to get around Havana without seeing things as they really are. Yes, there are tourists who only stay in the Old Town and visit the Tropicana and other tourist venues. But that is not what the students or

Tulane faculty do. They are there for a few weeks, and the "real" Cuba is hard not to see. It's in your face.

Further illustrative of this sad situation is the following excerpt from another, uncorrected, e-mail I received.

Dear Uncle Sam,

I am writing to apologize for all the terrible things which we Cubans have done to you while living in the United States. Please let me begin with my own humble plea for forgiveness.

Forgive me for being too Cuban, too Spanish, too European and too white. I know how painful it must be for you to have Spanish speaking Caucasians living on your soil.

Forgive us for paying our taxes and for obeying your laws.

Forgive us for being charitable and for believing in equality and social justice. Forgive us for helping the Nicaraguans and the Haitians in South Florida.

Forgive us for adding to your culinary diversity. Forgive us for our black beans, roast pork, arroz con pollo, arroz con mariscos, fried plantains, broiled red snapper, shrimp enchilado, Cuban sandwiches, flan, pastelitos de guayaba and a host of other dishes that lack the refined sophistication of your meatloaf.

Forgive us also for brewing coffee that actually looks, tastes and smell like coffee.

Forgive us our humanity. Please Uncle Sam, I implore you to forgive us for our participation in the political and civil life of your nation.

Forgive us for becoming U.S. citizens. Forgive us for voting in your elections.

Forgive us also for learning the lessons of Henry David Thoreau and Dr. Martin Luther King Jr.

I now realize that we Cubans are terrible people, and we have hurt you in unspeakable ways. But I assure you that we will get out of the country as soon as we regain our homeland. Unfortunately, it does not appear that this will happen any time soon; therefore, if I am so bold, could you please allow us to remain here just a little longer? I promise that we will do our best to behave more like a stereotypical minority.

There was no signature to this e-mail, but in many ways it did not need one as it represented the attitude held by many.

One morning just as I arrived at my office, I received a telephone call from a friend in the library letting me know that a Cuban American who worked at Tulane wanted to talk to me about my program and was at that moment headed towards my office. I was not enthusiastic, but I told my secretary about the imminent visit and to let me know when he arrived so that I could greet the visitor in the outer office and show him into mine. My visitor arrived in just ten minutes, and he was a very pleasant surprise.

Nearing retirement but looking a decade younger, Rafael Céspedes was one of the many green-suited employees in the physical plant of the university. He introduced himself, and began to share with me his experiences in Cuba. In the late 1950s, when he was a young man, he had been a journalist. He, at the risk of his life, had fought in the Revolution. It was not long after Castro's accession to power, however, that he saw that this was but one tyranny replacing another, and that the new tyranny, would be an even more restrictive and abusive one. Soon his attitude became known, and his reward for his efforts to create a better society was thirteen years in prison. Thirteen years in an abyss of anguish, abuse and despair, separated from his wife and family. Thirteen years of never knowing whether he would ever see freedom again. Thirteen years in which he could not care for his family.

When he was finally released in 1976, he joined his family, which had in the meantime wisely emigrated to New Orleans. For most of the past twenty years, he had been working at the university and remained active as a journalist and was a well-respected member of the dissident community. Listening to this, I braced myself for the inevitable vitriol from what was certainly one of Ortíz's ambassadors. Instead, I was totally taken off guard when he explained that he not only supported what the Institute was trying to accomplish, but wanted to help in any way he could. I almost fell out of my chair. Unlike Ortíz he believed that if people, especially students, spent time in Cuba, they would see it for what it was. Unlike Ortíz, he had not only fought for change, but had paid the price for it. Rafael would soon become one of my closest confidants, sharing with me his intimate knowledge of Cuban American culture, his keen political sense, and helping to let moderates know that, no, I was not a communist, and yes, we all wanted the same thing.

I was honored when he invited me to the annual picnic in Lafreniere Park organized by a local association of Cuban ex-political prisoners. Between mouthfuls of *congri* and succulent *lechón asado*, I met many who had fought to create an honest and democratic system in Cuba, and then found themselves spending several years in a hot cement room, often alone. Unlike their self-appointed spokesman Ortíz, these men and women, like a great many Cuban Americans, were, on the whole, moderates. Yes, many had hate and were angry, but there was also a strong element of gentility and wisdom. I also respected the fact that through all of this, their wives had stood by them. In fact, Rafael and his wife Rosa were about to celebrate their fiftieth anniversary. The other nice thing was that I now had some armor. If these men and women, whose credentials were impeccable, did not have a problem with the Institute, then perhaps it was Ortíz who had a problem.

Rafael's group, however, are not the politically connected ones. Probably few readers of this book even knew they existed. When Americans, and Cubans, think of Cuban Americans they think of the Cuban Right. They are not too far wrong. These are the Cubans who matter in American politics, and they frighten every class of Cubans in and out of Cuba, the communists and the anti-communists alike.

"Nick, let me tell you," my friend Amaury once confided, "when the change comes I am afraid of many things. There will be big changes. We have been in a shell since 1959. But we are as smart as anyone. If the Mexicans can compete, we can too. But it is the Miami Mafia who frighten us." We had been sitting in a corner of my favorite Havana paladar, La Esperanza, and here Amaury stopped and drank the rest of the red Chilean wine. We had completed our dinner. "They are on the winning side. Your politicians owe them. They voted for Bush and he won. If they had voted for Gore he would be president. But we can't stand another dictatorship, another Batista, another Castro."

CHAPTER 7

The Future

Things seem to be changing in Cuba, but little actually changes. Though older, Castro is still in power. Albeit weaker, the embargo continues. While more divided than ever, the Cuban American Right is still strong. This dynamic changelessness, for want of a better term has been part of the landscape for a very long time. After a long struggle for independence, the colonial chains to Spain had no sooner been broken than they were replaced by those of the United States. And no sooner had those been broken than Cuba was shackled to the Soviet Union. In fact, their dependence on the Soviets was even more binding than anything they ever had with the U.S., and what little economic diversification they had achieved was replaced by even more reliance on sugar. Now, in a world where autarchy is no longer feasible, they have their independence, and plenty of stagnation to prove it. When Castro becomes a memory, they will have an unprecedented opportunity to achieve their potential, one in which no doubt the U.S. will play an important role as a partner, both in trade and aid. Hopefully we, too, can learn from the past in our relations with Cuba. Clearly, American foreign policy should serve American interests, but it can, and should, also support Cuban interests. Our support for past repressive regimes there helped to create the present one. There is an undercurrent of pluralism in Cuba, and we should continue to focus on assisting its development.

And Castro will die. The Cubans and others will get wind of it when they see a massive troop deployment throughout the country for no apparent reason. When the news is out, hundreds of people and scores of institutions will make their move: the Cuban security services, the military, the U.S. government, the rightists throughout the United States. Assuming that he does not die first, Castro's brother Raúl is scheduled to continue the show, a new scene but not a new act. Not only is Raúl more of a hardliner than his brother, he lacks his charisma. If he does become head of state, as many expect he will, he might be able to keep things running for a while, but there are many pretenders to the throne and he is reputed to be less adept than his brother at managing different factions. While these may not move against Fidel, it is unlikely that they would show the same deference to Raúl, and he may be forced to accept some collective leadership arrangement.

The other thing is that this is not just palace politics. When Castro exits stage left, the people are going to want the show to be over. When the house lights don't come up, their simmering frustrations will boil over. As social unrest increases, it will turn up the heat in the ruling circle to either reform or repress, and consequently promote more internal divisions. A bloody crackdown or two may buy some time, but at the cost of much greater global isolation. If Raúl does ascend the throne, the stalemate with the U.S. will probably continue, unless he decides to lead a transition, which is unlikely. When Raúl is removed, through whatever means, the U.S. will probably quickly lift the embargo and seek a rapprochement. It is even possible that the U.S. would lift the embargo when Fidel dies.

Another possibility, which could evolve out of the first, is that a transitional "perestroika" government would be formed in Havana and welcome the U.S. initiatives. This could happen after, or instead of, a perhaps bloody effort of the hard-liners, with or without Raúl, to keep control. The perestroika regime could include leaders of the party, military, and security services, and could temper previous policies and be more open to better relations with the U.S. Basically they would be looking for an exit through which they would not be persecuted by the new regime. They could eventually go the way of much of the security services in the former Soviet Union, forming a new underworld of organized crime. In this scenario, compromises will be made and Cuba will eventually progress in the democratic and market-oriented way the Czech Republic, Poland, and Hungary have. Much though not all of its old intimacy with the U.S. will be restored, but this time, perhaps after a couple of years, as a member of NAFTA.

The old guard in Cuba is strengthened by the fact that Castro has been fairly successful in suppressing independent activity on the island. The result is that much of the cadre of alternative leadership is concentrated in the relatively small dissident movement. It is easy to forget your differences when you are sharing a cell or on the run, but when the opportunities for and rewards of leadership of the country arise, latent divisions will come to the fore. Internal divisions among the opposition will only strengthen the hard-liners, at least in the short term. The dissidents, however, have more moral authority than anyone on the island and, in the long term, will offer the best hope of reconciliation and progress.

Another possibility is that elements of the Cuban American Right will mount an attack without U.S. support or aid. This would bolster the old communist guard on the island, even though the Right would likely be thrown back into the Caribbean and another repressive government would likely be formed. Or they will form a beachhead and Cuba will see a civil war. Or, least likely, they will win and another repressive government will be formed. In any case, they would find little public support. The role of the conservative Cuban Americans has no parallels; nowhere in the communist world have successor governments had to deal with hundreds of thousands of exiles, many of whom were waiting to return and reclaim what once was theirs. The closest was in Germany, when some West Germans celebrated by driving their Mercedes through the Brandenburg Gate, running Trabants off the road, and lighting their cigars with East German money.

However things work out in the end, the Cuban American Right will take credit for everything, from the decades of pressure on Castro, to the sparks that led to the transition, to the plan for their new government. The blueprint for Cuba's future has already been drafted, in Miami. After decades of absence, of a near-total disconnect from the island, many will return, seeking not only to regain what they lost so long ago, but also to be the gatekeepers of the new society. When there are elections, many rightists will fund and try to manipulate them to ensure that their allies come to power, something they have plenty of experience in. They will do their best to see that they are the beneficiaries as the state enterprises are sold off, and they will try to make sure that the flood of cash coming in from D.C. and the private sector also passes through their hands.

Hopefully the actual future will not be this bleak, and many of the first generation Cuban Americans may be too old to be actively involved. Some will be content just to be able to go back and visit, at will, and maybe keep a house there, perhaps even their old one. Some will genuinely want to help Cuba more than themselves. And some will be involved in business but never really move back to the island. Even with this, there will be plenty of angry, vindictive people stepping off the planes, their bags filled with a half-century of rage. And it only takes a minority to make a mess of things. The Right will have some competition on the island, if past transitions are any indication: the Cuban security services, which employ thousands of people, will also try to make the transition, as outlined in the previous scenario.

It is important to realize that the United States has only limited ability to affect Cuba's transition. Its ability to do harm is greater than its capacity to do good. It is possible that we would send in the Marines, most likely with the fig leaf of United Nations auspices. If the Florida Strait becomes crowded with boats headed to the U.S., then the Marines are a real possibility. We would have a hard time absorbing hundreds of thousands of Cubans, and there would be pressure to do something about it, especially from the southern states, which would be most affected. Such a scenario could also be the product of baiting by the communist old guard, a last-ditch effort to go out in style as defenders of national honor. It would be bad news for everyone if we let this happen. We intervened before, and, despite our efforts, left in our wake a string of dictators, of whom Castro is only the worst and most long-lasting. Cubans need to move their history to the next stage themselves.

These different roads to change are not mutually exclusive, and while the Cuban Americans will play a role, the first and second paths of a hardline or transitional regime, perhaps sequenced, are the most likely. It is conceivable that Cuba could continue its competition with North Korea and Vietnam to be the longest running Stalinist state for some time to come. Clearly, as Cuba's history, and more recently Castro and the Cuban American Right, have demonstrated, fear and repression work.

Considering any of these possible political futures, it's a good thing that Cubans have a well-deserved reputation for resilience and resourcefulness. They are a tough people, and their creativity and penury have brought their entrepreneurial spirit to the fore, even if it is all done looking over their shoulders. There are some who will have a very hard time when the boulder is lifted from their backs. There is a tremendous need for training on how the market works, and how to make it work for them, but they already have a good bit of economic experience.

When things do open up, the magnitude of the needs in Cuba will be even more apparent to people than they are today, and expectations in Cuba will increase with the transition. First among the needs will be a new legal structure that deals with property rights: Land and other titles will be one of the first bones of contention. Fortunately, much of this ground has been covered in other formerly communist countries, creating such things as constituent conventions to write a new constitution, electoral procedures, government structures, economic policies, etc. Much of that is largely straightforward. There will be plenty of retooling, the training seminar business will be booming, and plenty of U.S. government dollars will fund it.

American business will also come in, and come in big. The material needs are so extensive it is mind-boggling. Start underground and work your way up: sewage disposal, water treatment and delivery, roads, the redevelopment and extension of the telephone system, upgrading of the electrical system, agricultural inputs, lumber and other building supplies, cars, heavy machinery, foodstuffs, computers. In short, you name it and Cuba needs it. Traffic will be a nightmare. The Malecón and an old ring road are the main thoroughfares; gridlock will be the order of the day. Crime will explode, as it always does when the pressure-cooker lid of a police state is lifted. If history is any guide, conflict and dissension will continue to shape events on the island. Those who have the most initiative and talent, so long repressed, will find their opportunities and rewards, and will be resented by those who prefer the languor of days gone by. Cuba will be a mess with plenty of opportunity.

And down the road, don't entirely write off the Communist party. Yes, they will be put to run, at least initially. As one Cuban said, the change will be like a *planadora*, one of the machines that strips away old asphalt on roads. The whole system, and much of the party that operated it, will be consumed by the road muncher. Those who had operated it for the past decades will see that they are suddenly underneath it, melted, broken, chewed and spit out. They will lie low for a while and let things take their course. Later, as in other countries, they will change their name, try to act a bit more hip, claim to have expiated their sins and hark back to the good old days, when there was no crime, when the Right did not throw their weight around, when Cuba was the master of its destiny. Or so they will say. Remember, not everyone there hates Castro. He has support in the countryside, where a lot of the resources have gone and where people are more conservative. There will be those whose careers and pensions depended on the party or the old state and who will be unable to make a transition to a democratic and market-based system; and there will be those who are not used to working for a living and will resent the fact that others are living better than the. People will expect continued quality primary educational and public health systems.

The waves of change will wash ashore throughout the region. American tourism to Cuba will explode, at least for a while, with disastrous consequences in other places that have depended on it. People will find that the Cubans are a wonderful, warm, informal people, with whom you can always strike up a conversation, and who are generally willing to share their thoughts with you. From the guayabera shirt to salsa music, it is an open, welcoming and thoroughly sensual place. Tourism is one of the largest foreign exchange earners in Mexico, and much of that depends on American tourists. Fewer American tourists will be getting off the plane in their shorts and sandals in Cancún, instead they will be going to Cuba to taste the nectar that the island has to offer. The other islands and places in the region that depend on Americans will suffer similar effects.

No doubt Cuba will receive preferential trade access to the U.S. Cuba and the U.S. are natural trading partners, and have a tradition of commerce that goes back to when both nations were colonies. More recently, the closure of the U.S. market and the fall of the Soviet Union have resulted in the development of extensive trade relations with many European and other developed countries. These relations will combine with and balance the strong trading relationship with the U.S. Many poor countries would be glad to have the opportunities which geographical proximity, access and cultural affinity to the U.S. offer.

Not only will preferential trade agreements be a subtle apology for the decades of the embargo, but we will also want to showcase Cuba as a success story, one that we can be proud of instead of nursing our wounded pride over. Trade agreements between the two countries will enable the development of the types of assembly plants, or *maquiladoras*, that are on the Mexican border with the U.S. now. Depending on the terms, some may even leave Mexico and relocate to Cuba, further affecting the Mexican economy. Smoke from Cuban cigars will billow from the U.S, wreaking havoc on other cigar-producing areas such as the Dominican Republic and Honduras. Americans will find that the Cubans are not only eager to improve their lives, they are hard, literate, disciplined workers who have an appreciation for quality, precision and punctuality.

There will be effects in the United States as well, not all of them positive. Sugar will be a contentious issue, especially in states such as Hawaii, Louisiana, and Arkansas. Either the import quota will have to be redistributed, to the chagrin of other trading partners, or it will have to be increased, which the sugar-producing states will fight strongly. Cuba and Florida will continue to have friction, at least partly over imported citrus products. Domestic tourism will also be affected, as, at least initially, many people will forgo domestic destinations to see the island.

Those states that are negatively affected, however, will find that the downside will be offset by other opportunities. In Louisiana, for example, jobs at the ports will increase with the exports coming downriver, and there will be an increase in demand for other products produced there, such as soy, cotton, beef, fertilizers and other petrochemicals. And if they play it right, New Orleans could be a good stepping off point for flights to Cuba and offer packages for both places. The same is largely true for Florida. If trade results in increasing competition for citrus and seafood, this could be offset by multi-destinational tourism, increased export activity and services. Texas and Louisiana will export their rice, the Midwest its grains.

There are some things we can do to facilitate a transition, and these actions should be taken today, without waiting for the confusion of an early post–Castro period.

One, leaders in both political parties should make it clear that though they sympathize with all of Castro's refugees, they will not force any government on the Cuban people nor will they permit American land and institutions to form a basis for such an effort. We've said it before, now we have to do it.

Two, people to people contact should continue to be encouraged. Business contacts should be facilitated. It may not be politically wise to end the blockade while Castro lives, but it should be progressively weakened.

The U.S. should follow these two principles for a while and then move forward cautiously in the early post–Castro period, refraining from threats or triumphalism. Cuba and the U.S. can be partners and friends. The cautious approach taken by the United States in Eastern Europe in 1988, '89, and '90 worked well.

The monistic impulse reinforced by Spanish rule still dominates Cuba, and the Cuban American community, despite the desire among a great many Cubans on both sides of the straits for a pluralistic system tolerant of differing views and a representative government that can be held accountable for its actions. The Cuban people have fought for well over a hundred years against the false harmony of monism and political and economic monopolies, against corruption, intolerance and repression. They have fought for a society in which power is checked, in which the media are free, and in which fear is replaced by an expectation of fair play and critical inquiry. But, thus far, they have lost the war and monism still prevails. Part of the reason is that opposition movements have often confused the representation of the problem — Machado, Batista, Castro— with the problem itself. In the end, only through a system in which a culture of tolerance and political and economic accountability prevails, and in which there is a rising tide of benefits for all, can Cuba unfurl its potential and sail out of the sea of strife in which it has floundered for so long.

Chronology

1492	Christopher Columbus lands on Cuba in October.
1511	Diego de Velásquez begins conquest of Cuba for Spain
1515	Conquest of Cuba is complete.
1538	Santiago de Cuba named capital of Cuba.
1542	Promulgation of the "New Laws," phasing out the *encomienda* system.
1607	Capital of Cuba moved to Havana.
1717	The Spanish crown establishes a monopoly on tobacco.
1740	Royal Company of Commerce is established, bringing Cuban commerce under a monopoly system.
1762	British occupy Havana for eleven months; trade flourishes.
1791	Cuban sugar and coffee production begins significant expansion due to independence war in Haiti, then called Saint Domingue.
1818	Spanish crown opens Cuba to international trade.
1850–1851	Departing from the U.S., Narciso López leads two unsuccessful expeditions to free Cuba from Spain and annex it to the United States.
1853	Birth of José Martí.
1868–1878	The Ten Years War initially led by Carlos Manuel de Céspedes seeks end of Spanish rule on the island. The rebellion ends with the Pact of Zanjón in 1878 when Spain agrees to limited reforms.
1879–1880	The Little War, led by Calixto García, who rejects Pact of Zanjón and is defeated.
1880	Spain begins gradual abolition of slavery, culminating in emancipation in 1886.
1895	Cuban independence war begins in February, militarily led by Generals Antonio Maceo and Máximo Gómez. José Martí killed in May.
1898	U.S. battleship *Maine* sunk in Havana Harbor in February. United

Information for this chronology is drawn from the following: Max Azicri, *Cuba: Politics, Economics and Society* (New York: Pinter Publishers, 1988), Juan M. del Aguila, *Cuba: Dilemmas of a Revolution* (Boulder: Westview Press, 1994), Louis Perez, *Cuba: Between Reform and Revolution* (New York: Oxford University Press, 1995), Jaime Suchlicki, *Cuba: From Columbus to Castro* (New York: Pergamon-Brassey's, 1986) and Jaime Suchlicki, *Historical Dictionary of Cuba* (Lanham, MD: Scarecrow Press, 2001).

States invades Cuba in July; in December, Cuba, Puerto Rico, Guam and the Phillipines come under U.S. control by terms of the Treaty of Paris.

1901   Platt Amendment, allow U.S. intervention, becomes law in U.S. and Cuba in February and June respectively, Tomas Estrada Palma becomes president in December.

1902   U.S. military forces depart Cuba in May.

1905   Estrada Palma reelected in questionable election.

1906–09   Estrada Palma, facing revolt by Liberal party in August of 1906 requests U.S. intervention, which lasts until 1909.

1908   Liberal party wins presidential election; José Miguel Gómez becomes president.

1912   Conservative party wins presidential election, Mario Menocal becomes president; reelected in questionable election in 1916.

1917–1922   U.S. intervenes to quell Liberal revolt against Menocal's reelection.

1920   Liberal party returns to power with election of Alfredo Zayas as president. U.S. exerts extensive influence on Zayas' administration. Sugar price drops from 22.5 cents to 3.8 cents.

1924   Liberal party retains power. Gerardo Machado elected president.

1928   Machado fraudulently reelected for six-year term .

1933   Machado ousted after widespread protests and loss of U.S. and military support in August. Military names Carlos Manuel de Céspedes. He is ousted in September when military uprising led by Fulgencio Batista installs Ramón Grau San Martín as president.

1934   After passing much social and economically nationalist legislation, Batista removes Grau in January and names Carlos Mendieta as president in January. In May, the Platt Amendment is abrogated by the U.S.

1935–40   Batista, as powerbroker, oversees administrations of José Barnet (1935), Miguel Mariano Gómez (1936) amd Federico Laredo Bru (1936-40).

1940   Promulgation of new Cuban constitution and election of Fulgencio Batista as president.

1944   Grau San Martín elected president as head of Partido Revolucionario Cubano (Auténtico) party.

1947   Eduardo Chibás splits from Auténtico party and establishes Partido del Pueblo Cubano (Ortodoxo) party.

1948   Auténticos retain power with election of Carlos Prío Socarrás as president.

1952   Fulgencio Batista organizes coup, becomes president.

1953   Attack on Moncada barracks in Santiago de Cuba by Fidél Castro and supporters fails.

1954   Batista elected to four-year term in presidential election in which he is the only candidate.

1955   Castro and others released from jail under provisions of an amnesty. He moves to Mexico and builds the July 26 Movement.

1956	Castro lands in Cuba; attacked by military which kills most of his forces. Survivors establish rebel base in Sierra Maestra mountains.
1957	Urban-based Revolutionary Directorate (DR) attacks presidential palace and radio station. The attack is repulsed and many DR members are killed.
1958	U.S. implements arms embargo against Cuban government in March, Batista launches unsuccessful military offensive against rebel forces in May.
1959	Batista goes into exile in January; Fidel Castro becomes Prime Minister in February.
1960	Cuban government nationalizes U.S. oil refineries in June. The following month the U.S. eliminates Cuban sugar quota. By October U.S. owned banks, railroads, sugar mills and other properties are nationalized and the U.S. institutes a trade embargo.
1961	Cuba and the U.S. end diplomatic relations in January; in April the Bay of Pigs invasion fails.
1962	The Cuban Missile Crisis occurs in October.
1968	All remaining Cuban private enterprises are nationalized.
1970	Ten Million Tons sugar harvest campaign ends with 8.5 million tons harvested; results in severe economic dislocation.
1976	Cuban government promulgates new constitution.
1977	Under President Jimmy Carter, U.S. and Cuba resume partial diplomatic relations with the establishment of an interests section in each country's capital.
1980	125,000 Cubans depart to the U.S. via the Mariel boatlift.
1989	Mikhail Gorbachev meets with Castro in Havana in January; signals beginning of end of Soviet assistance to the regime.
1990	The severe curtailing of assistance from, and trade with, the Soviet Union, and trade with Eastern European nations, leads to severe economic contraction in Cuba and efforts to develop tourism and biotechnology sectors.
1993	Use of dollars by Cubans is legalized by the Cuban government in December.
1998	Visit of Pope John Paul II in January signals loosening of religious restrictions in Cuba.
2000	Cuban child refugee Elián Gonzalez, rescued from the Florida Strait in November 1999, is returned to Cuba with his father in June.

Index